Life-Changing Explosion
of
Consciousness

Life-Changing Explosion
of
Consciousness

Introduction to
Holographic Psychology©

Margrit Spear Ph.D. / LMFT

To order additional copies of this book, contact:
Xlibris Corporation
1-888-795-4274
www.Xlibris.com
Orders@Xlibris.com
27593

Contents

Author Acknowledgment

My heartfelt thanks to Dr. James Pottenger for changing my life and for giving me the opportunity to create a book inspired by his life's dedication to research into human potential.

I would also like to express my gratitude to my first editor S. S. (who does not want her name mentioned), for accepting the challenge of editing my work.

Many thanks to the talented Xlibirs editors for their professional work.

A special thank you to my gifted cover designer Paul Lloyd Warner for creating a one of a kind design for my book.

Thank you Dr. Louis Nitti Jr. for letting me share your "Sam" graphic.

Additionally, many thanks to my friend Robert L. Satterlee for making me computer literate and for bailing me out of the many mysteries of computer language.

Dedication

This book is dedicated to all the people who dare to go beyond their current understanding and are willing to test their own unrealized potential. It requires the individual to take a closer look at his or her own beliefs that are keeping them stuck in their lives.

Important Message
to the Reader

It is highly recommended that the reader becomes familiar with the word interpretations contained in the glossary as misinterpretations of the words used to explain our principles can create confusion. Holographic Psychology introduces a new belief system that will change the world when the subjectivity of language use (interpretation) is realized. It is our hope that you test and implement the principles that gave Holographic Psychology its foundation and then report the findings to our research department.

Reports can be mailed, faxed, or sent by e-mail to:

Dr. Margrit Spear
PO Box 711
Jamul, CA, 91935

Fax: (858) 271-9236

E-mail: spear@mill.net

or:

Dr. James Pottenger Research Department
PO Box 711
Jamul, CA 91935

E-mail: jamesp@mill.net

Web site:http://www.simplyjoy.com

Note for the Curious Reader

In the preface we have incorporated an abbreviated synopsis of the principles that make up Holographic Psychology.

Detailed explanations follow preface.

Preface

Engraved in Holographic Psychology are the principles of universal laws governing every human being. Just as a hologram retains the entire image within each part, universal principles function within every person as immanent and transcendent consciousness whether the person is aware of this interrelationship or not. We can state that the part is in the whole and the whole is in each part, a type of unity in diversity and diversity in unity.

Holographic Psychology, an integration of ancient wisdom and leading-edge discoveries, is the brainchild of Dr. James Pottenger, president of an independent research team in Southern California. He and his research team have spent almost fifty years developing the dynamics of Holographic Psychology by examining psychology, philosophy, and religion, thus creating a synthesis of behavioristic, humanistic, and transpersonal psychology. Their system exposes that the above-listed psychological schools correlate with paradigm shifts within human consciousness, bringing into existence new levels of understanding that alters the individual's worldviews. These paradigm shifts expose three different levels of comprehension in which humans express their reality.

Our research labels these steps: first, the "reactive" or "physical" stage based on behavioristic psychology, or first level of comprehension;

second, the "mental" or "psychological" stage that first became psychoanalysis focusing on the individual's past and his/her conditioned or inherent pathology, which later became humanistic psychology or second level of comprehension; and third, the "transpersonal" or "spiritual" stage that became transpersonal psychology or third level of comprehension, focusing on the location of a human's preexisting potential pushing for actualization.

Within these three worldviews, levels, or stages, the observer "sees his or her world" from differing perspectives. Many people have experienced some of these stages at one time or another; however, we find that currently on planet earth the majority of individuals express their lives from the "reactive" or "physical" stage of first-level comprehension.

Within this reactive or physical stage, the object of blame is outside the individual, where someone or something else is responsible for our circumstances and our feelings. Realizing that the causal factor to reaction is an internal psychological evaluation is new to a first-reality understanding, yet it was practiced centuries ago by giants like the Buddha, Jesus, and later the philosopher Spinoza. For example, Jesus taught that the Kingdom of God is within, but first-level people are not sufficiently developed in their awareness to comprehend and test his true meaning. Realizing where comprehension takes place will change our therapeutic approaches to healing and will eliminate victimhood. Location of Comprehension is our internal or "inner" realization referred to in German as "Feststellung." This shift in perception will change our world because it makes available the unlimited potential of the collective consciousness from which we are never separated. Our focus is utilizing the potential lying within the individual that is unlimited in its expression and is encoded in universal consciousness.

Dr. Pottenger has been involved in metaphysical teachings for decades. He was a personal student of Ernest Holmes and his brother Fenwicke Holmes. He is continuing their research and is bringing to light the complexity interwoven within the individual's psychological dynamics. He holds a doctorate in metaphysics and an MBA in systems analysis. He has been CEO of numerous businesses.

As a teenager, he spent nine months in a coma, and if it had not been for his mother's unrelenting search for alternative treatments in the metaphysical field, he would probably never have recovered. Experts in traditional medicine had no solutions and provided no hope for him to ever recover from his comatose state of being.

Holographic Psychology is a revolutionary change from traditional psychology as its focus lies in the potential of the individual instead of on his or her pathology. Included is an invisible element called universal consciousness that can be empirically tested.

Most of the world's population today still lives in a first-level comprehension where discoveries of second-and third-level comprehension are unknown and cannot be understood until a shift in awareness takes place. Consciousness interrelated to universal laws is excluded from a first-level vocabulary. Consciousness is still mostly misunderstood in our culture as this aspect of human nature is invisible, has no tactile construct, is not part of an audible format, and has been largely labeled unscientific because it cannot be duplicated in a traditional laboratory setting. It can, however, be tested and verified by the individual.

When we begin to comprehend that consciousness is the foundation of all existence, our lives will drastically change. Consciousness or the mental aspect of a human becomes significant with second-level comprehension because the individual is awakening to the mental realm existing within his or her physical body.

Third-level comprehension exposes how consciousness acts through involution and evolution/teleology as preexisting potentials within human beings. This means that when third-reality or the transcendent aspect of consciousness is discovered, it is realized as a universal consciousness expressed according to the different levels of understanding.

In this book, we will answer many questions humans have argued about for centuries and explain the difference between innate versus environmental causes. As consciousness evolves, so does our current level of understanding. As we become familiar with these universal principles governing our existence, we begin to realize the complexity contained within ourselves and our universe. Our biggest change in comprehension will be the realization that meaning in life is expressed subjectively and not objectively as believed for centuries. The subjectivity will be recognized as psychological dynamics of a human being, expressed at his or her current level of comprehension. When this realization dawns, our research labels it "Location of Comprehension" or "Feststellung." This realization presents a quantum leap in understanding in which the individual becomes aware that language is a symbolic means that is interpreted subjectively and is not based on other people, places, or things, as it is based on the individual's current self-image. The individual realizes where any word or feeling interpretation takes place (meaning inside him or her) and is consequently no longer a victim of his or her environment.

Self-help systems have contributed significantly in empowering individuals by changing culturally adopted beliefs that formed our habit patterns. Few of these self-help systems include the monistic principle of third-reality in which the potential is actualized as preexisting within a human being. What has rarely been realized before by mainstream Western cultures is that our beliefs shape our reality, and how we express this reality has to do with whether or not we understand how we work psychologically. When there is no awareness that our life is more than multiple biological functions directed by the brain, it is impossible to integrate preexisting mental or transcendent principles governing our existence.

The importance one's mind plays is discovered when the individual awakens to second-level comprehension. Prior to that level, the individual operates in the behavioristic stage that is based on an objective (external) world, believed to be the cause of his or her state of being. In this first level, "mind" is a synonym for the brain. The belief system of the individual is heavily based on cultural indoctrinations where the individual is trained by his/her primary caretakers and mentors.

In this book, the principles contained within Holographic Psychology are explained in detail and a glossary is provided defining the specific levels of comprehension and particular word meanings, including functional definitions that are empirically testable.

As we begin applying second-level comprehension in our daily lives, enormous changes affecting our relationship to the whole world are noticeable. Experimenting with these principles provides a way of living an actualizing life of empowerment. When these principles are fully integrated into our daily existence, they provide the basis for a healthier, happier world in which the individual thinks and acts with multiple options. "I-thou" becomes a common practice facilitating a win-win situation for all.

Background Information of the Writer

My personal connection with Dr. Pottenger came as a result of a last attempt I took to reconnect with my daughter on a healthier basis. We three met during a seminar in a mountain retreat in the summer of 1993. At that time I was a successful psychotherapist, but to my chagrin, I was unable to reach my own teenage daughter. This state of being brought sleepless nights and days filled with worry. I lived through numerous bouts with her running away from home, with abuse, with attempted suicide, and with defiance in general. As a single mother, I was at my wit's end. None of my coworkers in the counseling field had satisfactory solutions to my problems. The fact that I was able to change countless people's lives but was unable to help myself and my daughter to a much greater level had a traumatic effect on my life.

During this mountain retreat, in sheer desperation I hoped that my daughter would be able to connect with her spiritual self and hopefully find a more positive way of living. She attended this retreat against her will and made sure that her interactions with her mother were minimal. What was supposed to be her turnaround became my salvation, which liberated me from my constant worries. The more I had worried, the worse the situation had grown. I had no idea that my worries contributed a substantial degree to our painful situation.

For years I had been an avid student, eager to learn about psychological advances, new concepts, and advanced studies in general. Metaphysical teachings had always intrigued me and somehow I felt intuitively that they could hold the key to a more beneficial life. I had attended countless seminars in hopes of finding the missing piece to the puzzle promising Nirvana. I was seeking out leaders in the field and healers of all sorts in hopes of attaining ways that would magically transform my way of life, as my life was a bowl of cherries but most of them were sour.

As a last resort, I was referred to a renowned psychic reader in hopes of finding the missing piece. Although I was very skeptical, I went; and she told me that there was nothing I would have to do, attend, or see, etc,. She stated calmly that when I was ready, it would come to me. I was furious at that time, thinking that this session was a real waste of my time and money. I reasoned that if I weren't ready, why would I even seek advice? It made no sense at that time, and finally I got to a place where I told myself "the hell with it all." I had been seriously searching for decades in books, in seminars, in tapes, in different groups for a connection that would deliver a so-called Nirvana or peace of mind.

My life up to that point was consumed by work. There was no social life to speak of, and I generally worked seven days a week for years. Often I traded between three different jobs to sustain my family as I had no outside help or any financial support for my kids or my higher education. When this supermother syndrome became unbearable, I became more and more discontented. I blamed the change in the economy; I blamed the lack of money, work situations, and the world in general. The more I worried, the worse my situation grew.

Help finally came when my latest job ended, and I became unemployed for the first time in my life. Now I was forced to take time to sort through a half century of activities called my life. As I looked at my goal list, I discovered that most of my desires for pleasure had never been fulfilled. Although I succeeded educationally despite the fact that everybody told me what I had in mind could not be obtained in my situation, I eventually made it. After I got divorced, I decided to go back to school full-time to attain a PhD in psychology, a field that had always interested me. As a former pharmacist, I dealt with the medical side and with time became more and more disturbed with what I witnessed. Often I felt that the cause of the person's problem was met with a mere Band-Aid and that the real problem was either covered with pills or was never fully addressed.

Besides work and school, taking care of my two children, house pets, and garden appeared to be an endless job. In retrospect, I do not know how I succeeded but with sheer determination I made it. Thinking back about the struggle I endured for years makes me feel tired today.

I met Dr. Pottenger at the brink of my collapse. As we began to exchange stories, I became very excited about what he shared because I felt that I had finally found a fellow traveler who had similar philosophies and ideas. I wondered if perhaps he would have the missing piece to my puzzle and indeed he did. For the first time he explained to me how psychological dynamics govern my life. In disbelief I felt as I had been hit by a brick. Dumbfounded, I wondered why in all my years of study I had never come across these principles. Rather than working on the pathology of the individual, his principles utilized the potential which is lying dormant in most of us. This radical change of approach altered my life forever and also changed my career perspectives. It further improved the interaction with my children and provided a much saner environment. I would have never believed his answer even five years earlier as I was trained to find solutions in external causes and not in internal belief systems.

My latest job included working with the homeless population, the schizophrenics, drug-addicts, and alcoholics. Prior to that work, I spent three years solving problems in a crisis center. I was also an academic and psychological counselor in a junior college and completed various other internships. To become licensed as a Marriage Family and Child Counselor required three thousand hours of internship alone. By now, I was tired diagnosing what was not working in the individual, and I was often self-critical when the person appeared unable to understand my carefully-thought-out plan for recovery. I felt responsible for the world and indeed carried this heavy burden on my shoulders.

In time I began to wonder how I could have been so blind for so long. I don't know how many times I had heard the phrase that the secret to success was "inside," but I could never find the location of that "inside" (my brain, my heart, my body) to make total sense of it. I practiced very little meditation because I was unable to shut off my racing mind and gain a peaceful state or stillness.

With renewed hope and a much better understanding, I joined Dr. Pottenger's research organization and have been working with him ever since. It has been the most eye-opening experience, and it has changed my life forever. During his many years of research into the fields of psychology, philosophy, and religion, he has written numerous observations and began to divide humans into three different realities relating to their world and themselves.

I have attempted to transcribe his philosophical observations and explain them in a way so that the reader can obtain a better understanding. The theory can be tested empirically and when comprehended, will change the individual's life forever. Happiness will be the realization that life is an internal job in which humans become directors of their own psychological dynamics that govern their beliefs. One of the biggest benefits includes the individual's capacity to referee whether to buy into unpleasant feelings or not. With this capability, the individual will no longer be a victim of his or her circumstances and the quality of his or her life will change forever. Health will be viewed as an interconnected component of the individual's thinking and feeling, and prayer and miracles will be understood as tapping into a preexisting potential or universal consciousness that is available to all of us.

Life will be viewed as a continuum of change with opportunities for growth. The level of our mental capabilities will be determined by our level of understanding. "Who am I" will be explained on the basis of three different realities. As we gain awareness, we will begin to realize the awesome principles that govern our entire existence. Discoveries in mental capabilities will be validated by discoveries in the scientific field of research such as quantum physics. Shifting into different levels of understanding means transposing the foundation of our reality. Our self-esteem will change and will provide a healthier self-image. Life in the next century will be viewed very differently and the search for "salvation" or fulfillment will be understood not only by the elite but by mainstream citizens. How long it will take for this transformation is anyone's guess.

Ten years ago we could have never predicted the success of an Internet. As we interact globally, we will advance more rapidly and realize that people around the world are also connected with the same universal consciousness. Granted we will still speak different languages and have different customs but our psychological dynamics are identical whether we are Jewish, Catholic, Protestant, Hungarian, Spanish, or Mexican.

We live in exciting times and as the individual wakes up to the realization that life is an expression of "inner" dynamics that produce his/her outside world, we will enjoy a very different state of being. We will realize that when we express thoughts and feelings negatively it will bring negative results and possibly illness. On the other hand, positive experiences bring positive results including better health and a happier life. Relationships will improve drastically as imperfections and complaints are realized as "inner" states of awareness that can be controlled and replaced with beneficial options. The quality of life will no longer depend on mom, dad, the government etc, but will be realized as a function happening within the individual. The objective world illusion that is perceived to be external from the individual will still dominate for a time but as greater awareness within the human being is awakened, we will enjoy a different world. Perhaps, the biggest discovery will be a realization that in each one of us lays the secrets to illumination. Motivation for attaining this state of being will be determined by the individual's biological DNA and his or her spiritual DNA. In time, science will realize that not all advances are testable in man-made (external) laboratories. Our mental laboratories will yield the most profound advances and the greatest surprises. Until we wake up to an understanding that knowledge is innate but also transcends our physical bodies, little will change. Authorities don't like to be told about an existent component they had not been aware of.

Rewriting history will include our so-called past but will also expose an evolutionary teleological process that is continually changing humans. Former habits or beliefs based solely on survival will be viewed as having been necessary steps before attaining new insights and directions. We won't have to belittle limiting beliefs regarding our past since they played an important part in discovering our new insights. Expanding our boundary lines takes courage as perceived uncertainty often creates shivers and produces fear. Had it not been for courageous individuals we would never have advanced in most fields of endeavor with the speed we have.

Leading-edge discoveries have always been prone to criticism by traditional perspectives but unless a person tests new hypotheses, they will remain simply hypotheses. "Fake it until you make it," is an excellent slogan since all potential does preexist within the individual as it is embodied in universal consciousness. As a confirmed critic and skeptic, I would never have believed that changing my understanding would change my life and the life of everyone around me. It has, and I am eternally grateful for this amazing discovery.

Learning to understand the psychological dynamics is like learning a new language. In the beginning, we feel awkward since our habits have dominated our life to date. How we acted and reacted was predominantly based on what we were told to do or not to do by authority figures that had "the truth." Questioning our existence takes courage and a form of curiosity to discover new ways of being. Challenging our beliefs is not as easy as it sounds. Unless we actually practice a different way of thinking and feeling, we will never experience our new ways of being. Each person is different and there is no guarantee in any of the endeavors. Accepting our psychological dynamics as our main source of evaluating our reality is difficult for most as this means redirecting our currently believed information. Our brain still plays an important part in our existence but the brain is fueled by the universal mind. Imagine that our brain is like the hard disk of the computer and the mind is the software. Without the software directing the hardware, we do not get a functioning program. As we become more familiar with the awesome mind principles, new insights are revealed to us.

Learning to respect the universal laws is of utmost importance since these laws produce our beliefs and our actions. When the mind is on the forefront of interest and discovery, we have a different world as the previous discoveries will be viewed as stepping stones to our current reality. We have only begun to discover the most profound truth that was revealed to Buddha, Jesus, and many other avatars.

Our research organization does not claim to have the only solution for discovering consciousness. We have, however, incorporated a component called "Location of Comprehension" or a "Feststellung" that will be most significant and to our knowledge has never been revealed in any literature.

Rather than presenting the dynamics contained in Holographic Psychology in scholarly writings only, we have attempted to make them a functional course that can be tested by each person. Unless the reader is motivated to test these universal principles, s/he will never locate where the foundation of real learning takes place. Level three comprehension in one hundred years may be equivalent to level one understanding of many thousands of years. Our greatest gifts are imbedded in the mind waiting to be activated. The journey of discovery will be the most rewarding task we have ever encountered. There are no promises for instant change to be obtained from books or tapes since this discovery is a self-discovery, motivated primarily by our spiritual DNA. As our awareness is directed into our "inner" life, it will mirror our state of being as our outside world. The more peaceful we are the more peaceful our world will be.

Since this information is new to most people, we have attempted to give multiple explanations and have repeated the essence of this discovery whenever we felt it appropriate. We realize that the dynamics are complex and may not be comprehended by everyone. These life-changing dynamics will not come forth by simply reading this book; they have to be personally tested. Intellectual knowledge is the first step to a greater wisdom, but actual experience holds the key to dramatic life changes.

We wish you much success.

Glossary

Holographic Psychology: the birth of an evolutionary process of understanding that consciousness is part of the individual's psychological dynamics.

These individual dynamics are formed on the basis of either their behavioral (first-level understanding), humanistic (second-level understanding), or transpersonal (third-level understanding). It is the process within evolutionary history, motivating the individual to attain perfection and is part of the discovery that our beliefs are subjective in nature, therefore manifesting in our lives according to our current level of understanding.

Holographic Psychology is the recognition that we are all part of an unlimited potential that is capable of being realized by every human being. The essence of Holographic Psychology deals with universal laws that have been previously discerned mostly by mystics. It is the capacity to separate objective and subjective language describing our realities. When this recognition is fully realized, we label it Location of Comprehension or Feststellung (a German word encompassing objective and subjective realization) arising in second-level comprehension, representing a quantum leap in understanding (see Location of Comprehension.)

The self in Holographic Psychology is part of a preexisting wholeness, expressed multidimensionally through levels or stages of understanding, i.e., first, second, and third level. When Holographic Psychology principles are realized, victimhood is eliminated as the new level of awareness enables the individual to choose between beneficial and harmful experiences. Mastering the theory of Holographic Psychology eliminates boundaries that have been limiting human beings for centuries.

Consciousness: the awareness of one's own existence, a function of the mind; the full activity of the senses and the awareness of something or someone thinking; the way in which the individual understands his or her reality; the absolute coherent law of correspondence both immanent and transcendent; that which exists as vertical time meaning now, having no past and no future; an invisible energy which has always existed and will always exist; is the soul that never dies; the basis or matrix of all existence. Consciousness is a multidimensional flow of divine intelligence that operates through the brain but is not confined within the brain. Consciousness functions within our mental activities whether we are aware of this linkage or not. It is not definable as a traceable substance that can be calibrated or validated in a scientific laboratory. It is however testable in our own mental laboratory reflecting our state of mind, based on our current level of understanding.

Dualism: the basic belief that one's conscious awareness is separated from the understanding that is giving meaning to his/her reality. A doctrine believing in two independent sources such as genetic ("inner") *v.* environment ("outer"). The belief in separation between body and mind, body or person and environment. Dualism exists before a person awakens to the verity that his or her reality is psychologically evaluated (as a result of his or her current belief system) and is not the consequence of another person, place, or thing. Reality is based on belief systems and not on someone's definitions.

Note: in order to move out of first-level comprehension, it is required that an individual understands the difference between an external or "outer" cause orientation and a psychological or "inner" evaluation.

Ego: the decision maker or the conscious awareness of our internal driving forces; it is the part of the individual that makes the distinction between self and environment; it is part of our self-esteem that has a sense of individuality and a self-conscious awareness producing an individual's current reality or current self-image. This decision-making capability does not exist in first-level comprehension, since the "I" or "self," capable of refereeing his or her own psychological dynamics, awakens with second-level comprehension.

Guiding principle: that which unfolds within us, a psychological, spiritual-type DNA, patterned at or before birth, bringing into existence our level of fulfillment in life. This invisible essence is part of being a human. It transcends and includes our physical body and our environment. This guiding principle can also be called panentheism in philosophy which likewise holds true for some theologies including mysticism.

Inner: the recognition of one's own beliefs and experiences that are subjective in nature, the individual's psychological dynamics rather than an effect of his or her environment; a conscious identity of the self that awakens with second-level understanding, the awareness of the mental realm or consciousness that is not recognized in first-level understanding. It is a comprehension we label "Feststellung," the realization that observes who or what is doing the observing.

"Inner" is a state where "being" produces "doing." "Inner" in third-level comprehension means being aware that a universal transcendent power is part of, and working through the individual. It is accessing the invisible powers called omnipotence, omniscience, and omnipresence.

Note: Changing from an outer to an inner orientation brings with it a paradigm shift in understanding that cannot be taught. It can only be realized and tested experimentally. This increase in awareness has to take place within the individual and is an awakening of his or her mental capacities. The "I" is actualizing his or her own potential.

First-level comprehension or behavioristic psychology: the term which traditionally refers to a controlled stimulus followed by a conditioned and predictable response. "If I follow the given instructions, I arrive at the correct answer." The process involves observed behavior and is performed in the absence of conscious awareness or any other mental aspects. The world of the individual is based on materialism related to environment and is observed objectively without introspection. Reality is based on external objects or subjects forming a particular pattern (habit) believed to have conditioned the brain. This external or outer oriented conception regarding subjects or objects is what we name first-level comprehension or first-reality understanding that is based on a survival level originally created by our ancestors.

Second-level comprehension or humanistic psychology: the science of mind or the research of consciousness that began as a science in the 1960s and was spearheaded by psychologist Abraham Maslow. He introduced the science of human potential and his research involved knowing, understanding, and fulfilling the needs of an individual through self-actualization, based on the preexisting potential within each individual human being. It is the birth of an awakening self. This paradigm shift is the basis of second-level understanding that began in the late nineteenth century as a metaphysical teaching by transcendentalists such as Emerson and Madam Blavatski who became the founder of theosophy.

Third-level comprehension or transpersonal psychology: conscious awareness that also transcends the person. It is the science of spirit and its correlation to mind and consciousness; the investigation of relationships between religions, philosophies, linguistics, and psychologies; the realization of a unified ground of being that has always been experienced in mysticism. It is part of the individual's connection to his/her environment and universal mind that Carl Jung named the "collective unconscious." We name it the birth of third-level understanding.

Note: an individual capable of realizing this third level of comprehension is able to understand first-and second-level reasoning, but a person in first-level understanding is not capable of comprehending second or third-level reasoning.

Location of Comprehension or Feststellung: Feststellung (a German word encompassing objective and subjective realization) arises in second-level comprehension, representing a quantum leap in understanding. This Feststellung provides freedom to consciously referee our thoughts, feelings, and actions we refer to as options. When we act from this second level of comprehension, we are aware that we are responsible for the way we feel (either good or bad). The concept is based on a realization that the individual's language exposes his or her current level of comprehension. The self in Holographic Psychology is part of a preexisting wholeness, expressed multidimensionally through levels or stages of understanding i.e., first, second, and third level. Practicing Location of Comprehension eliminates victimhood and enables the individual to choose between beneficial and harmful experiences. It exposes the subjective process of language psychologically as one's current belief that is based on the individual's accepted habits. It is the realization that consciousness is subjective; that meaning given to one's world is within his or her own understanding and it brings to light that his/her level of awareness determines his/her experience based on his/her own self-image. It is the place within consciousness that determines either to continue or change current beliefs that are justifying the individual's worldview and his/her relationship with others. It opens the doorway to a capacity for realizing that there may be a collective Source existing that includes the separate self and provides preexisting potential for change to every person capable of understanding and testing this principle. Location of Comprehension is a major key for shifting a human's reality, influencing its potential for actualization.

Location of Comprehension is the most challenging paradigm shift because it collides with the beliefs that the individual acquired while functioning in a first-level understanding. It is the realization that locates where personal reactions to everything take place. It is the recognition that comprehension of any situation takes place **within** the individual. Therefore, it presents a giant leap in understanding because the individual is now capable of eliminating frustration and consequently enhances his or her state of health. It diminishes fear of former established beliefs instilled by our mentors such as, "If you don't do this or that, you will go to hell." When we implement this principle, we determine and take personal responsibility for the outcome of the meaning we ascribe to and the feelings we experience in any given situation. Never before have we been told that what we give meaning to is psychological, is who we will believe we are (what we have accepted and learned from our parents and authorities), and is how we think and react. Realizing the subjectivity of language creates a form of liberation and empowerment from formerly believed dogmas that were prescribed by other people.

Options: the ability to make different choices regarding former habits or reactions. Instead of getting angry over a situation, the individual will consciously choose a beneficial rather than a toxic reaction. The individual has realized that anger is activated within him/her and is not, as formerly believed, a reaction that is caused by the other person, place, or thing.

Outer: the conscious awareness of a reality that is based on the meaning of an objective world that is external from the individual. It is the belief that the senses relate to the individual's environment which is the responsible cause of his/her experience. The individual's worldview is based and determined on cultural beliefs that were handed down from generation to generation. Belief is largely accepted on the basis of authority figures that establish and decide the meaning of truth. It is a state where doing produces being. For example, "The harder I work, the sooner I will be rich."

Preexisting potential: the awakening of Source awareness that is part of a collective consciousness, both innate and transcendent, within each human being. It is a conscious participation of the cosmic law in action, that which reveals the truth to the extent the individual is capable of understanding the unfolding of creativity in any given field. It is a force that is invisible, nontangible yet can be tapped into in a relaxed state of mind. Geniuses like Mozart, Beethoven, Picasso, Michelangelo, Einstein, and numerous others were capable of tapping this level of intelligence. Many mortals have been capable of experiencing glimpses of this altered state of consciousness and the results have often been reported as out-of-body experiences or near-death experiences. During this state our reality is altered as it connects with a level of consciousness for which we generally have no reference point. As a result of such experiences many people live different lives. In the past, most people would have never shared their experience for fear that they would be branded strange or even insane.

Every person has an innate potential, but not every person is capable of developing their inherent potential to its fullest capacity. We believe that the extent to which we develop our awareness is a spiritual blueprint that is decided by a "higher" or more intelligent force existing within consciousness that is both immanent and transcendent.

Psychological dynamics: the mental processes of physical and/or mental drives existing within the individual's consciousness that are both immanent and transcendent. They are patterns of growth and development determining the individual's level of motivation which expose boundaries that mirror their current self-image i.e., the beliefs s/he has accepted as truth. These beliefs are part of our cultural conditioning that is handed down from generation to generation. It is where the individual exposes his/her evaluation process that is prompting him or her to act either positively or negatively regarding every experience. Instant reaction based on first-level comprehension utilizes responses believed to be conditioned by the brain. Choosing actions arises from actualizing preexisting potential of second-level comprehension where the "I" is awakened. This concept is unknown in first-level understanding as motivation is believed to be based on a brain that has been conditioned. It is the moment in which the individual understands that his or her evaluation process is subjective in nature. It is an empowering realization that allows the individual to choose to react either positively or negatively to any situation and is the basis of his/her evaluation process. In second-level understanding, the individual is capable of analyzing his or her reaction to any situation because s/he is now aware how and where his/her "inner" dynamics are experienced "before" producing his/her behavior.

Refereeing: a subjective decision-making process that is activated in second-level comprehension, allowing the individual to choose deliberate options to any reaction. It is the individual's capability to respond favorably or unfavorably to any experience; the capability to separate **meaning** from **feeling** as aspects of one's own psychological dynamics that are located within the individual exposing his or her current self-image.

Self-image: the idea and the conception of the individual's mental image that is subconscious and validates his/her current belief system. It is part of the decision-making process that is formed in the subconscious mind and determines the basis of his or her own self-acceptance and the state of being that is projected into the world.

Note: the role a self-image plays is not known in first-level comprehension.

Self vs. self: "Self" with a capital *S* means universal consciousness, the essence of all creation; "self" in lowercase means within human consciousness. Human consciousness does not equal universal consciousness yet is part of universal consciousness. Universal consciousness is the umbrella or the foundation for levels of consciousness humans utilize.

Soul: There is no soul awareness in first-level comprehension. In second-level understanding, a human's soul is an extension of spirit, an invisible form of intelligence and energy receiving inspiration from the "inner" world of consciousness and impressions from the "outer" world. Soul is subjective and mirrors the person's current level of awareness. Soul is the individual's consciousness that emerges out of spirit, our transcendent divine essence functioning in our individual consciousness. Our human bodies contain spirit and soul. Soul is conscious yet also subconscious. In third-level comprehension, soul is synonymous with spirit. Soul survives the physical death of the body as it is part of an eternal Source of intelligence and energy.

Spiritual DNA: a blueprint that is created by a "higher" intelligence determining the life lessons of the individual. Encoded within this pattern is the level of motivation with which the individual will function during his or her life. A person will either be motivated to gain greater levels of education and life experiences in general or will be happy in a job that is supervised by some authority either sacred or secular. An example would be the difference between an employee and an employer. An employee is generally required to "follow" someone else's instructions. An employer is required to make decisions and test the results of his/her decisions.

Differences in motivational levels are necessary as we need all the various professions to make this planet work. We believe that these patterns are encoded before or at the time of birth. Our biological DNA still plays a very important part in the development of a human being but we believe that it is intricately connected with the spiritual DNA. How this spiritual DNA is formed or the level in which it is expressed in the individual is a major part of our research.

Subjective: the meaning and experienced feeling the individual projects to the outside world. It is where conscious awareness interprets data with the resources that are available within that person; communication is based on the individual's current level of understanding. It is the assumed knowledge of the individual's conscious awareness as distinct from the object world itself; where an option or potential is capable of being actualized. It is not part of first-level understanding where awareness is reduced to the functions of the brain.

Truth: as expressed in third-reality, is the absolute of mysticism or transpersonal psychology; that which is perceived by the soul-mind as functional knowledge of a system of values produced within the individual. It is that which is workable for us and resonates with us, an intuitive matter we accept and learn to test.

Truth in Holographic Psychology is expressed in three different levels. In first-level comprehension, the individual's beliefs are dualistic such as a separation between religion and science or mind from body. In religion, it is believed that not everything is matter but there is no way to prove that assumption. In science, we have a monistic approach in which everything is believed to be reducible to matter. Science in that view rests in materialism. In second-level comprehension, the individual believes in a material universe that is perceived and evaluated mentally and accepted as truth, i.e., the evaluation will be what the individual believes is truth. In third-level comprehension, the individual is capable of experiencing the collective wholeness as truth (there is no separation between "inner" and "outer"/external reality as comprehension is now located as a subjective evaluation).

Truth, of the "I AM" or wholeness is the high essence a first-level comprehension labels as a separate God. Our mental nature is something we discover within ourselves and later realize that it is both immanent and transcendent. It is not something we get from someone else as it preexists in universal consciousness as potential awaiting actualization.

Holographic Psychology

Overview

Before we fully introduce you to Holographic Psychology, let us mention how it was named.

A hologram is a three-dimensional image and when we take a single laser light and split it into two beams, each individual part will still contain the whole picture. This image can be split over and over again and will continue to retain the entire image. So is consciousness within the human being. Humans cannot be separated from consciousness whether they are aware of this interconnection or not. Consciousness plays an integral part as the individual changes his or her level of awareness, beginning with second-level functioning. Consciousness bears similar characteristics to a hologram and thus we created the fitting name: Holographic Psychology.

Holographic Psychology celebrates groundbreaking concepts pertaining to an awakening individual self; it is about finding his or her individual voice that has been asleep and is now ready to test new areas of being. Furthermore, it is about experimenting with the subjective world existing within and also apart from our own consciousness, beyond our five senses, corresponding to the way we evaluate our own thinking process. It is about testing how our meaning reflects our understanding, thus revealing our reality.

As our perception changes so does our meaning. Life is therefore an ongoing school that has no ceiling since the quality of our life depends on our own level of awareness. As our awareness soars so does our understanding. As our understanding increases, it brings with it inner peace and contentment. Our state of inner peace and contentment is in turn reflected to the outside world, which also benefits from these positive states of being. It is a realization that we cannot separate the understanding of our world from our consciousness and neither can we be separated from the consciousness of the universe. Separation is only a form of innocence (ignorance) we inherited with a dualistic world model. When we practice a unified principle, also called the collective or universal unconscious, we are actually learning how each individual can consciously create a healthier, happier world that benefits everyone.

As we realize that we are all connected in consciousness, our lives change in many ways. We are no longer victims of our environment but are individual beings, refereeing the values we have currently accepted and the part we play in the world. After awakening to increased levels of consciousness, victimhood is optional. Playing the role of a victim will be the result of refusing to wake up to our "inner" potential that is available to all of us.

Holographic Psychology shows a synthesis, exposing three different levels of comprehension. They are first-level understanding, meaning the "reactive" or "physical" stage that became behavioristic psychology, second-level understanding or the "mental" or "psychological" stage that first became psychoanalysis focusing on the individual's past and his/her conditioned or inherent pathology and later processed into humanistic psychology. The focus in humanistic psychology is on the potential of the individual rather than his/her pathology. And finally, there is the third-level understanding, the "transpersonal" or "spiritual" stage that became transpersonal psychology focusing on the location of a human's preexisting potential pushing for actualization.

Within these three worldviews, levels, or stages, the observer "sees his or her world" from differing perspectives. Many people have experienced some of these stages at one time or another. However, we find that currently on planet earth the majority of individuals express their lives from the "reactive" or "physical" stage of first-level comprehension.

Changing from one level to the next, i.e., from a behavioristic level of understanding to a humanistic level, must be viewed in the context of "movement" from a present level of conscious awareness to a new or different level of conscious awareness. Processing this change involves realizing that we have something to do with the way we react and feel about any situation. The discovery of this correlation is what our research calls "Location of Comprehension" or "Feststellung." It presents a quantum leap in understanding and will change the way the individual views his or her beliefs and behavior forever.

Counseling therapy in particular will undergo major changes with this theory because after realizing the subjectivity of language, the individual will have options to create life-changing experiences, using his or her new gained empowerment for actualizing desired change.

The essence of Holographic Psychology is based on an invisible intelligence and/or energy called universal consciousness that is, however, empirically testable by every human being. Since consciousness is the foundation of our theory let us get familiar with its essence.

What is Consciousness?

The definition of consciousness is baffling for most people in first-level functioning and, without an increase of awareness into a second level of comprehension, is neither understood nor comprehensible. Consciousness has always existed but has not been part of our everyday awareness orientation. Mystics have been aware of this existing mental aspect of the human nature for centuries, and it is reasonable to infer why these mystics were unable to explain something that has no foundation or reality in the everyday life of a first-level person.

Consciousness is the awareness of one's own existence, a function of the mind; the full activity of the senses and the awareness of something or someone thinking; the way in which the individual understands his or her reality; the absolute coherent law of correspondence both immanent and transcendent; that which exists as vertical time meaning now, having no past and no future; an invisible energy which has always existed and will always exist; the basis of all existence.

Consciousness is a multidimensional flow of divine intelligence that operates through the brain but is not confined within the brain. This consciousness acting through the brain of the human is not separated from the transcendent, and whether it is named after a thousand different gods, it is still linked to the same Source (Self) that is responsible for all creation.

When a paradigm shift in awareness happens, we no longer experience a separation from God or our Source. Over two thousand years ago Jesus taught that the Kingdom of God exists within. Neither his disciples nor the general population were able to grasp what "within" really meant. For years, I wondered where this within was supposed to be, and I kept on chasing for answers. Until I finally realized how consciousness is expressed, I was wondering if it was existing within my brain, my soul, or some other specifically designated place in my body. The harder I tried to find this "kingdom" somewhere, the more frustrated I became because it appeared that no one in my current circle of people had a satisfactory answer for me.

Consciousness signals the birth of a transcendent awareness that awakens within the self as being part of the Self. Self, with the capital S, means universal consciousness, self, with a lowercase s, means within the individual human consciousness. Consciousness functions within our mental activities whether we are aware of this invisible process or not. It is not definable as a traceable substance that can be calibrated or validated in the laboratory, but it can be empirically tested.

How exactly consciousness divides or is separated into the different levels is currently being researched. The more we become aware, the more we realize the complexity of everything. Reality is not simply black or white when we advance in comprehension. We soon learn that the majority is gray and has infinite expressions. Living fully in third-reality may be centuries away for the masses, but as each person becomes more aware of consciousness as a whole, this planet will change much more rapidly.

In third-reality existence, we will no longer have wars, famine, sickness, etc., as we will have learned through testing in second-reality the wonders already preexisting as human potential within consciousness. A dualistic worldview is now realized as a level of consciousness in which the individual is outer oriented, expressing a limited self-image. It is not wrong. It simply reflects a limited reality. Living and feeling the interconnection of all existence is life changing. Spending time alone is never viewed as being lonely but is a necessary ingredient for keeping in tune. Radio stations, like consciousness, are transmitting at all times, but in order to receive their signals, the receiver must be in tune.

Third-reality consciousness allows me to understand second and first realities, since I have now realized that a different answer simply means that the individual works from a different level of comprehension. I can understand level two and one, but I also realize that level one cannot understand level two or three. Awakening to preexisting wonders is my birthright, and where it will take me is not my concern since I feel totally guided by a power that is much grander than myself.

Within each one of us exists a treasure chest, and in order to utilize its treasures we have to wake up, become more consciously aware, and allow this infinite guidance to show us the way. The consciousness that makes the tree grow and expresses as a particular tree, i.e., chestnut, walnut, or sweet-gum is the consciousness that motivates us to be who we are. This motivation is a level of consciousness and the use of this consciousness can differ in every person. We can't force changes in others; they have to awaken within themselves. We have the intelligence to live in harmony on our planet, but we have to be able to first let this intelligence unfold within ourselves.

Consciousness is not merely a change involving objects or a new system of measuring facts or quantities. It is a change that has to take place within our own conscious awareness. Our actions and reactions are based on how we interpret our psychological dynamics. As long as we keep reacting to our world, we have not yet realized that the subjective nature of our reactions is caused by our belief.

As we witness our psychological evolution, miracles can be a daily appearance. We are truly unlimited beings and the only limit we have is the one we put on ourselves. We do of course have physical limitations such as how hot the water can be before we get burned, how much we can lift, etc., but I don't believe that consciousness stops evolving at some point.

Much confusion exists regarding soul as it is often viewed as a separate entity that has entered our body. Soul is universal consciousness within the individual that is connected with spirit. It is not separate from the individual or universal consciousness. This invisible form of intelligence and energy receives inspiration from the inner world. Soul survives the physical death of the body as it is an extension of spirit that is part of an eternal Source of intelligence and energy.

We can view human nature as a soul that uses a body to access higher spiritual realms. Many theists believe that the human body is a prison of the soul. However, after awakened conscious awareness, it can rise to a conscious awareness of its universal spirit. When this extension to universal intelligence remains bound in the human body, it will operate with a belief of separation as body and soul are viewed as two separate components existing independently of each other. This concept is difficult to grasp when there is no awareness of consciousness that is both immanent and transcendent.

In the early myths, cosmic consciousness was exposed in gender terms as "Father and Mother." Regardless of which gender was used, the experience was not in the father or in the mother but in the one and only Source. Father in ancient civilization could be expressed as the left-brain function of intelligence, and mother or right-brain function represented creativity, caring, and love. After third-level awakening, these aspects, i.e., "male" (directing the intellect) and "female" (birthing creativity) are realized as left and right hemispheres of the brain that are contained within every person and will no longer serve as mere labels representing gender names that operate separately.

One of the most exciting areas in the twenty-first century will be the investigation of consciousness. As we begin to accept the notion that we are more than a body with five senses, we will be able to experience a reality that we never thought was possible. This acceptance will provide more room for questioning our own beliefs and habits that have limited us in so many ways.

We will incorporate a brief history of our own evolution that will give a better understanding of how what we believed became facts. We live indeed in exciting times and never before have ordinary humans been able to investigate and participate in the secrets of the universe because in the past the so-called authority figures made all the decisions for us. We have to recognize today that the decisions they made were based on their own level of understanding. In the past only an elite group of people were privileged to learn the mysteries that were revealed by prophets like the Buddha and Jesus. Regardless of how much we may deny a connection or are unaware of it, we cannot be separated from this universal Source that is reflecting our beliefs.

As our awareness increases so does our understanding of the laws that govern this universe. Despite enormous scientific advances in many fields, our current knowledge regarding consciousness is in a prekindergarten stage. Dealing with invisible energies may sound like a fairy-tale approach to a first-level comprehension yet as we begin practicing the laws of the universe by activating that which we want, we will tap into the preexisting potential instead of feeding our old habit patterns that do not necessarily serve us. By practicing what is beneficial to us, we will experience tremendous changes in the quality of our everyday existence. For example, rather than hoping that we don't get cancer (where our subconscious focuses on cancer), we will acknowledge our perfect state of health on a daily basis. This positive attitude and gratitude can play a major role in a person living a healthy life. Our nutritional factors, our time for rest or exercise, the company we keep, how happy we are in our job, etc., also play a major part in the overall state of health. Most people do not honor their body. They take better care of their pets and their cars than of the intricate system that sustains them. The intelligence that runs our body is absolutely phenomenal and enormously complex. As we become more in tune with our body, it will tell us what it needs. When we ignore the warning signals, we have to pay the consequences sooner or later.

Part of discovering Holographic Psychology has to do with understanding the importance the individual's belief system plays and where the seat of his or her belief is located. Holographic Psychology will explain why some people are eager to change their lives and others would rather die than change. By realizing the location of our own evaluations, some of the greatest benefits will be elimination of anger, frustration, jealousy, etc. and the celebration of an increased state of health. It means discovering that the world of the individual self is mirroring his/her self-image or self-esteem. A change in awareness will benefit the individual regardless of how old s/he is. It is never too late to experience the laws of the cosmic consciousness.

Holographic Psychology is one of the greatest discoveries for maintaining happy and healthy relationships. After locating its dynamics, victimhood is optional as the individual will have the necessary tools to referee his or her current state of emotions, therefore feeling empowered and in charge of his or her life.

Holographic Psychology entails a realization process in which the individual becomes aware that s/he has something to do with the way s/he thinks and feels. It is a new way of living by consciously participating and choosing whether to react or not react to any given experience because reactions are now located subjectively within the person. Blame no longer plays a part in his or her repertoire as the individual now has located the basis of his or her empowerment. This self-acceptance can also bring instant healing and/or improve health, as the focus of the individual changes from a codependent state to an independent state of being. With greater understanding, the individual will realize that formerly held beliefs can be changed. In a first-level understanding, the individual would not be aware that s/he has options available for change, because s/he believes that s/he is relating directly to the world.

Holographic Psychology is immediately testable by each individual and can create win-win situations for all. There is no need for a guru or a master as each person learns to practice change within themselves. There is no limit to exploring the holographic principle and it bears no hindrances to either culture or race. This holographic principle is timeless and can be adopted at any age. You don't have to go anywhere (India or some specified retreat) to master it as the key for adaptation is within you. After awakening to the principles involved, the many benefits include: better health, happier life, greater self-esteem, more energy, and one is capable of experiencing unconditional love. Realization of these universal principles reduces crime and most importantly the individual becomes aware that s/he is already connected with a Source that is capable of delivering his or her desired state of being.

Holographic Psychology is now capable of introducing ancient dynamics from a Western perspective, changing the psychological format forever by explaining the differences between the three levels of comprehension making up human understanding. Most importantly, a change in level comprehension means a change in the individual's reality affecting his or her behavior.

Principles of each level of comprehension will be explained separately as major functions of behavioristic, humanistic, and transpersonal psychology. The progression from behavioristic to humanistic to transpersonal level of understanding is what created this teaching. What we have learned from the previous stages (behavioristic, humanistic, and transpersonal psychology) is invaluable and enabled us to move forward to Holographic Psychology. We recognize these different schools of psychology as building blocks for attaining "higher" levels of awareness. (The reason higher is in quotation marks is that there is no so-called higher or lower in a third-level understanding. More about that later.) Comprehending level two and three cannot be taught per se, as they are the product of an awakening mind that has to unfold within the individual. Level-three comprehension can understand level two and one; however, level one comprehension is not capable of understanding level two or three.

Despite a realization that the majority of the population is still functioning on a behavioristic or first-level reasoning, there is a steady increase noticeable in what we would call the application of self-help systems.

The basis of self-help systems is part of second-level awakening where the individual can recognize that s/he has something to do with the way s/he perceives and relates to his or her reality. Reactions are now located as a part of the subjective process and the individual will notice differences in thinking and feeling in the areas where he or she applies this new-found wisdom. For example, an individual that will mentally practice seeing (and feeling) herself daily in a new job, better work conditions and more pay, can find herself signing a new contract with a new company often within his/her desired time frame. This change is due to practicing what we want on a daily basis, rather than practicing daily what we don't want or what is missing in our lives. Manifestation of desired changes depends on our own level of acceptance.

Celebrating this self has created an enormous self-help business in the West in which the individual learns that s/he is an important link to attaining or maintaining happiness. We call this realization the awakening of the personal self. There are dozens of approaches and their methods are similar. Seminars that have been introduced by groups such as Life Spring, Insight, Avatar, and Est have been responsible for helping individuals create new or different self-images. All methods introduce changing behavior by replacing old beliefs with new. Taking an interest in the self eliminates being a victim of someone else and is the beginning of what we name second-reality understanding. Taking charge of one's life means a quantum leap in understanding. This intermediate step (between first and third-reality practice) is very important as it brings to light limited boundaries to which the individual has been bound.

In the West, self-help books, tapes, and seminars have contributed greatly to a healthier level of self-esteem and a happier life. Erasing this step of recognized individuation by replacing it with a master can create difficulties for the Western seeker as the confusion between a personal self and a cosmic Self would most likely not be understood. The cosmic Self contains the individual self as a level of understanding but the individual self is not the sum total of the cosmic Self.

As we can notice by now, Holographic Psychology presents a paradigm shift changing from an external or objective world recognition to an internal subjective reality where the Source of all existence is realized as a collective base that is innate in nature. It entails the acceptance of a preexisting potential that is omnipotent (absolute power), omnipresent (everywhere present), and omniscient (knowing all). It is the most important discovery of science in the late twentieth century, revealing that the self-image is part of a process of human perception that evolves through three different realities, changing the person's belief system through conscious participation. It is a realization that the senses do not give us meaning and feeling regarding our so-called external world. What we witness or "see" (sense), which is external from us, is not the cause of our frustration but the meaning we ascribe to that sensed experience. For example, mom, our boss, or society will no longer be the focus of blame when we recognize that the seat of interpretation is within us and is not caused by mom or the boss, etc.

Practicing happiness will bring more happiness and practicing anger will bring more angry situations. Keeping our thoughts and feelings focused on what is beneficial to us rather than detrimental becomes a full-time job in the beginning, as our old habits keep rearing their heads. Without the increased awareness of second-level comprehension, we will not recognize that our thought process has slipped into an old habit pattern. Keeping vigil of how we think and feel is vital in order to implement our new found wisdom.

Holographic Psychology reveals, therefore, that the world is perceived within the individual and this perception is based on the capacity of the individual to interpret meaning. To illustrate this principle let us simply take the word "love." The meaning of love is as diverse as people. To one person love means to be hugged and taken care of; to another person love may include other aspects such as getting gifts, doing something special or doing what they love. For one person, feeling loved may simply be a personal way of getting attention or nurturing a specific sentiment and for another it may include not only his or her own needs but also the needs of others. Love is not simply a factual statement but is an evaluation that takes place within the individual. What feels loving has different interpretations. Love is not only something we receive from someone else but is a reflection of our own state of being. The more we can nurture our own sense of being, the more secure we feel and the more we can give to others. When we realize that love is an infinite flow of a particular energy or vibration, we will also realize that there is no ceiling to how much we can utilize this cosmic flow. When love fills the body, it emanates from us and touches those around us. Compare, for example, a state of feeling loving with the flow of water in a hose that is kinked versus one that is fully open. When it is kinked, water can only drip through it, and when it is fully open, we get a powerful stream. When we practice love unconditionally, we tap from a Source that has no limits. When we measure "tit for tat," we practice limited states of being.

This example does not express nor justify the wide variety of interpretations but attempts to give you a better understanding how word interpretations (the psychological dynamics) of each person can differ. The biggest difference will be experienced when the individual realizes that love is a feeling that is a reflection of his or her "inner" dynamics rather than an aspect or a function that is derived from other people, places, or things.

Many of us have heard at one time or another that we create our life. For the person with orthodox belief, this is a blasphemous statement since their life is in God's hands and not their own. From this first-level comprehension, this would be true since God is generally believed to be a being that is separate from them.

Creating our own life makes more sense when we move into second-level comprehension because we begin to understand the invisible cosmic laws that govern our existence. Our spiritual DNA will still unfold according to its blueprint, yet with second-level comprehension we will have learned that we have options for changing undesirable feelings. By now, we also realize that what we think and feel is what we create in our life. The ability to change what was previously not recognized as being changeable makes us directors of our lives. In first-level comprehension, we would still believe that we are victims of our circumstances. From an advanced second-level or third-level comprehension, we realize that we are never separate from the Source that is often called God.

♥

Much discussion frequently rises over the belief that some people are born with exceptional talents and others with physical hindrances. Why would someone enter this earth plane with physical hindrances when they might never before have had the chance to practice perfect health? The answers are numerous. However, in general, we mostly point our finger to Karma which means that we are reaping in this present lifetime what we had sown in a previous one.

From a Holographic Psychology perspective, we can entertain a different notion because we believe that there is a preexisting intelligence possibly deciding our fate even before we are born. Our research has discovered that there is both a preexisting intelligence and a preexisting potential within cosmic consciousness.

Mystics have long been aware of these universal dynamics and have been able to utilize them. Yet the general population has never been cognizant that such forces even exist. This preexisting potential is the awakening of Source awareness that is part of a collective consciousness, both innate and transcendent within each human being. It is a conscious participation of the cosmic law in action; that which reveals the truth to the extent the individual is capable of understanding; the unfolding of creativity in any given field. It is a force that is invisible, nontangible yet can be tapped into in a relaxed state of mind. Geniuses like Mozart, Beethoven, Picasso, Michelangelo, Einstein, and numerous others were capable of tapping this level of intelligence.

Many humans have been capable of experiencing glimpses of this altered state of consciousness and the results have often been reported as out-of-body experiences or near-death experiences. During this state, our reality is altered as it connects with a level of consciousness for which we generally have no reference point. As a result of such experiences, many people live different lives. The experience of this nonordinary state of being revealed life changes in their current existence. In the past, most people would have never shared their experience for fear that they would be branded strange or even insane. Today, however, we have worldwide research dealing with these phenomena.

Every person has innate potential but not every person is capable of developing this inherent potential to its fullest capacity. As noted earlier, we believe that the extent to which we develop our awareness is a spiritual blueprint that is decided by a "higher" or more intelligent force existing within consciousness that is both immanent and transcendent.

As humans we cannot add or subtract from cosmic intelligence but with greater levels of awareness, we can utilize more of the preexisting potential. To provide you with an example, let us take the letters of our alphabet. Identifying each letter separately is not the same as being able to combine various letters to create words or write about observations. Geniuses always utilized the preexisting potential to a greater degree than the average person who is not aware of this potential.

Again, we sincerely believe that each person enters this earth plane not merely with a physical DNA but also with a spiritual DNA. Experimenting with this intelligence and preexisting potential is a core aspect of our research. It cannot be randomly duplicated or validated in the laboratory, because the subject's level of awareness plays an intricate part. However, empirical testing seems to verify our proposed hypothesis. This pattern expresses within the subjective nature (consciousness) of the human being and unfolds accordingly.

A preexisting blueprint appears to determine the individual's level of understanding and ultimately creates the sequence and lessons for learning during a person's life. With this hypothesis, we are capable of explaining why one person is motivated to learn and investigate and another person is happy watching television without ever reading about a leading-edge discovery. The motivational level of each person differs, and this difference is expressed in a life pattern that is either active or inactive, such as a person entering college to become a scientist or the person happily delivering newspapers all of his/her life. Neither is right or wrong as it simply represents the level of awareness and motivation with which the individual came into this world.

Thus we have found that the individual expresses his or her life within boundaries that are based on the current level or pattern that is governing the individual's decision-making capability. Because of this inherent pattern, we can notice differences in the individual's motivational level responsible for creating change. An unfamiliar experience along with uncertainty is often scary for people with low inherent motivational levels because uncertainty generally produces fear.

When we analyze fear, we begin to comprehend that the letters actually stand for fantasized experiences appearing real (FEAR is actually F-fantasized, E-experience, A-appearing, R-real). Fear appears predominantly as the person's real self rather than their self-image based on his or her beliefs. When we translate this statement, we could say that fear is accepted as an inseparable part of the human rather than an accepted belief. We also have to be cognizant that in first-level comprehension there is no conscious "I" that is capable of evaluating current beliefs or initiating a process of change.

Understanding that the preexisting potential (spiritual DNA) of a child determines his or her curriculum in life will make child-rearing for responsible parents much easier in the future as they will realize that lack of motivational drives within their child may be part of his/her current life plan.

Frustrations can occur particularly with motivated parents who are raising unmotivated children. It is difficult to accept that the child's life plan (encoded in his/her spiritual DNA) may be entirely different from that of his/her parents (or the desires of his or her parents). Often, feelings of having failed to raise the child properly can linger for years and create subtle or not so subtle feelings of guilt. Guilt is a form of negative emotion that robs our energy. Children that are forced to perform or follow the footsteps of their parents often become depressed, run away, or commit suicide. Being a shining example is always beneficial but does not necessarily change the original blueprint of the child. We can't change persons, they can only change themselves. We can however be good examples. The easiest way to accept this predicament is to allow each person to unfold his or her own potential. The degree to which this potential unfolds may not be what we consider the norm, yet it plays an important part in the "soul" development of the particular person.

We are researching why and how each child becomes the person they are destined to be. Although we currently have many hypotheses that are capable of predicting certain traits, we are still investigating what it is that programs a person's DNA prior to his or her birth.

Our biological DNA certainly plays a major part, yet there is so much more to be discovered in the realm of human potential, including how we relate to each other. Our spiritual DNA expresses in the way it is informed by cosmic consciousness.

As parents learn how they and their children function psychologically, upcoming generations will be taught differently, and this difference will include the importance consciousness plays in our lives. The future will encompass the realization that we can change how we feel and thus eliminate being a victim of one's current circumstances. New generations will realize that life is an inside job that manifests on the outside. By outside, we mean anybody and anything that is external from the person. Our outside world is realized as a mirror image of our thinking and feeling. These processes have always determined the quality of our lives and as we consciously practice change, we will eliminate countless so-called maladies that are plaguing our current generation. Health will be realized as an important state of mind along with body functions where the focus of health will be on education including preventive treatments rather than focusing on the pathological nature of the human being.

Sickness in most cases originates in the mind and then manifests in the body. It is not the body perpetuating illness; it begins with our state of mind. As the mass consciousness (or race consciousness according to Ernest Holmes) changes, we will have a different world in which cooperation will reign over competition. It will no longer be our country against other countries since consciousness has no boundary lines separating, for example, Greece from the United States. Although our languages will still differ, the principles that make up Holographic Psychology will not differ regardless of whether we live in Chile, Mongolia, or in the United States because the foundation of everything is this invisible element called consciousness that is of the same Source within every human being. Fear is fear and faith is faith in every culture.

How we work with these principles is not simply a matter of taking a course but is an awakening that has to take place within the individual. We can intellectually understand many dynamics but the mere intellectual understanding is not necessarily life-changing. We can for example read affirmation cards on a daily basis for the purpose of changing undesirable habits in our life, but unless we connect with the feeling located in our subconscious level (that will change our circumstances), it will be just words that are espoused from an intellectual level of understanding. It appears that lasting change has to be programmed on our subconscious level or at least the Alpha level of brain waves. Our ordinary speech is executed on the Beta level of brain waves. Differences in which these states function are indicated with cycles per second. The lower the cycles per second, the more relaxed we become. Much research is happening in the area of brain waves and exciting results have been gathered, for example in the area of dyslexia or attention-deficit disorder where many people have been able to live "normal" lives after receiving treatments containing specifically designed brain-wave sessions.

Where Do Miracles and Healing Originate?

We are discovering that this preexisting potential is responsible for what we call miracles. Miracles happen when we tap into the level of consciousness that preexists and knows only perfection. The same principles apply for healing. Healing is connecting with the perfection of the essence we truly are. Healing takes place when we get out of our rational thinking mode connected with dualism and consciously unite with the perfection of universal consciousness that is linked to every person, every animal, and every existing thing. This connection may not be consciously known by many people. If, however, we cannot be disconnected from a potential perfection within consciousness, we are potentially capable of enjoying the results regardless of conscious or unconscious knowing. Healing is practiced in many modalities, and whether it is the shaman, the priest, sound, color, therapeutic touch, or simply laying on of hands such as Reiki (including the medical doctors), it is founded on the same potential perfection principles contained within universal consciousness, available to every person.

Healing will be examined in greater detail in our question and answer section.

A Pivotal Point That Altered Traditional Psychology

Psychology as a form of science that studies human beings and what produces their behavior has only been developed over the last one hundred years. Therapy prior to the last fifty years was mostly focused on an individual's problems. Family therapy (involving every member of the family) has been in existence a mere fifty years. A major breakthrough came in the 1960s with the introduction of humanistic psychology facilitated by a psychologist by the name of Abraham Maslow. Prior to that time, the focus of psychology dealt predominantly with the pathology of the individual.

For the first time, Maslow investigated healthy individuals determining what made a person happy and successful. He established a hierarchy for actualizing the individual's potential and stated that in order for an individual to grow, certain fundamental needs had to be met. His five drives consisted of (1) psychological (hunger, thirst, shelter), (2) safety (security from physical and emotional harm), (3) social (friendship, affection, belonging), (4) self-respect, a healthy ego) (5) self-actualization (taking responsibility for doing things).

It is clear that when we are hungry and have no place to sleep, we are not concerned with matters pertaining to a more spiritual life. Solving the problem of finding food and having some place to sleep would take priority and this priority is what he called the "basic needs."

Since that time we have witnessed many different approaches to psychological treatment. Yet the majority of treatment never included the importance of consciousness or the mind plays in human behavior.

Our research provides a synthesis of the three major schools of psychology (behavioristic, humanistic, and transpersonal) as they continue to play a significant part in our evolution. Now we need to become familiar with one of the most significant psychological aspects of a human's awareness which we named "Location of Comprehension" or "Feststellung."

Practicing Location of Comprehension means utilizing a reflective ability that observes and evaluates our current experiences. This inner or subjective functioning ascribes meaning and feeling to every experience and subsequently we consciously participate in producing our behavior. The result of our behavior is then not based on a cause that originated in the person's environment but is a psychological function that is actualized within the consciousness of the individual.

The realization of this aspect awakens within the individual in second-level comprehension and is not something that can be taught in a classroom environment. We can, however, give you a description of it. Let us take a closer look:

Location of Comprehension is a focus shift in which a person is consciously aware of his/her current self-image and the behavior this self-image is producing. It provides a means for testing new options to conditioned beliefs that in the past may have innocently created nonbeneficial outcomes for the person. To give you an example: the person may have been focusing on his or her ill health without having been aware that this focus produces more ill health. A new focal point would entail practicing good health thereby producing different feelings. In the beginning, this change in focus takes enormous conscious participation as it is generally foreign to our current reality. Experiencing change means testing new levels of awareness. By awareness we mean that humans develop a greater level of understanding (paradigm shift) in how they work psychologically thus participating consciously in universal forces that have always existed. These universal forces mirror our current beliefs. Therefore, when we focus on ill-health, we get more ill-health, and when we focus on good health, we get more good health.

How Does Holographic Psychology Differ from Conventional Psychology?

Holographic Psychology is an abrupt change from the customary behavioristic psychology because its focus lies in actualizing the potential within the individual rather than feeling controlled or victimized by his or her environment. Recognizing that habitual negative habits may be harmful to the individual's state of mind is generally not yet widely known. Holographic Psychology can make the individual aware that his or her reality can be changed by examining his or her belief systems.

Even today's behavioristic orientation is still dominating most cultures. It is where the object of blame is outside the individual, where someone or something else is responsible for our circumstances and our feelings. Realizing that the causal factor to reaction is due to an internal or "inner" psychological evaluation is new to a first-reality understanding yet it was practiced centuries ago by giants like the Buddha, Jesus, and Spinoza. For example, Jesus taught that the kingdom of God is within but people expressing first-level comprehension have not yet a sufficiently evolved level of awareness to comprehend or test its true meaning.

Realizing where Location of Comprehension takes place will change our therapeutic approaches to healing and will end the belief that the cause for unhappiness in the individual's life is based on "external" circumstances. Holographic Psychology principles eliminate the middle man or the subject or object of blame as the individual begins to realize where his or her feelings and interpretations take place. The psychological principles have to do with unfolding hidden talents that have been asleep perhaps for decades (preexisting potential) rather than deliberately focusing on areas that do not work beneficially for the individual. What is often expressed as pathological behavior emerged from limiting beliefs that were accepted and then nurtured on a daily basis. These beliefs created a current reality (self-image) for the individual and subsequently justified their behavior or situation.

Labeling an individual's illness can resemble branding a cow. The brand identifies the proprietor and the cow is now the property of a particular owner(s). If the individual believes that his or her label justifies his or her behavior or lifestyle, so it will be until s/he begins to question his or her acceptance of the biases that accompany the labels. For example, if the individual believes that his or her inability to deal with his or her state of mind is strictly due to a biological cause, there will probably be no further inquiry into alternate sources of cause. This individual will most likely adhere to his or her given diagnosis and take medication to aid his or her discomfort. (There is no awareness that many so-called biological causes may have deep-seated, mentally-created belief patterns that are working against the person.) Justifying circumstances is still based on a first-level reality that makes decisions from "external" observations or circumstances without being aware that these "external" observations express "internal" evaluations.

Let Us Examine a Pitfall We Are Prone to, When We Are Not Aware of How We Function Psychologically

The principles involved in Holographic Psychology can reveal the way we understand our own psychological dynamics, once we have gained second-level comprehension. Difficulties often arise when two individuals communicate from two different stages or levels of comprehension because the meaning and feeling they ascribe to the same words have different personal interpretations. Each individual may think that the other understands their point of view from their level of comprehension. When there is no awareness by either person that their subjective understanding differs, it can create frustration as neither person will fully understand what the other one is talking about.

For example, when Sam speaks about initiation, s/he recollects a vivid picture in his or her mind fitting a process and specific feelings associated with a particular ceremony of time and place where s/he experienced a shift in status or a formal admission to a society or a club. To Dale, initiation may simply mean having bought a membership in a particular club where s/he wrote a check to cover the dues. Neither interpretation is right or wrong since it merely exposes the individual's personal inner level of understanding.

Without this additional awareness, one person can easily assume that s/he knows what the other person is talking about, i.e., Sam can easily assume that Dale is capable of interpreting the word "initiation" with the same mental faculties and feelings s/he possesses. Unless we verify personal interpretation, we may exchange with a totally faulty conception and later wonder why we were not able to achieve consensus.

Unless I recognize possible differences in interpretation, I can feel irritated because I had assumed that the other person was capable of interpreting the given meaning the same way I did. Before my awakening to these differences, I used to think why would people litter the parks, streets, and freeways? Why would they not pick up their trash and dispose of it properly? The answer is, of course, that if others communicated on the same level of conscious awareness as I do, all trash would be in the trash bin and not on the streets.

Motivation for change is an innate pattern. Because of this inherent pattern, we notice differences in other people's motivational level that is responsible for creating their behavior. Some people are eager to change and experience new challenges and others will live out their existence on this earth plane with the beliefs s/he accepted from his or her mentors. As stated earlier, implementing an unfamiliar experience along with the uncertainty it brings is often too scary for people because it can produce a considerable amount of fear.

Frustration also arises from expecting that every person is capable of implementing change. When assuming this notion, we believe that they can adapt to our current level of understanding, which is often different from theirs. From our perspective, we assume that they will benefit and experience a happier life by accepting our principles, our views, and our general way of being. However, this usually well-meant assumption cannot be implemented or applied unless the individual is motivated to change and accept a different way of relating to his or her world.

When a different perspective is presented to an individual, it is usually either rejected or it awakens a process of inquiry. Comprehending the concept of level differences helps explain why this is the case. The inherent pattern that the individual has been given at birth may or may not make such comprehension of difference possible. Research proves over and over again that we cannot change other people. They can only change themselves. What we can do is provide a method for change when options to current beliefs are requested, but any method remains a theory until it is tested and applied by that person.

As new stages or levels of comprehension awaken, we will experience a different life because we are no longer trying to change the other person. We have become aware that each person can only express their state of being from the understanding they are currently practicing. Unless people begin to question how and why they relate to their life as they currently do, they are usually not aware that options exist to their current positions or situations. In that case change means changing the world and not themselves.

♥

The Importance of Belief Now and Then

Belief is a key factor that cannot be underestimated in gaining desired results. Belief has to be felt and is not simply a function of verbal expression or thought alone. The intensity or sincerity by which we are capable of believing will determine much of our outcome. If a person has unfaltering faith and believes with all their might, the results will manifest much quicker than the person that has to analyze every detail and ponder upon its validity. Belief is so vital in every area of life. If we believe that we are capable of tapping into the unlimited potential (that exists within all of us), we will have a different perspective from believing that our deeds and our life is limited because we were born black, white, Mormon, or Catholic.

Imagine what will happen when we teach our children that their own potential is unlimited. Granted we do have a limited physical life span on this earth but our soul/spirit or the amount of consciousness that is expressed in each individual human being never dies. Fear of death can be troublesome when we have no understanding of the Source that eternally exists in all of us.

When we look back in history, we can notice that belief in salvation later (going to heaven) is what kept slaves alive in those ancient days because their daily living conditions were in most cases unthinkable in the eyes of our current Western standards of living.

Today we have the necessary understanding available to create heaven on earth. Heaven in today's interpretation will not be a future physical place but rather current functions of our own personal understanding as we realize that we are an intricate part of a universal consciousness that has always existed and will always exist. When we are capable of living with the understanding and the feeling of this realization, our lives will never be the same. Rather than feeling isolated, separate, or lonely, we will realize the connectedness that invokes our soul. When we don't involve our feelings, the desired state is merely an oral representation of our mental wishes. Oral repetition regarding desired outcomes is helpful, but in order to get quicker results we have to include feelings as if we have already reached our desired goals. (Fake it until you make it.)

Children are masters in expressing feelings as their favorite block is not simply a piece of wood but represents a fire engine or Superman, etc. Their reality is based on their imagination triggering the necessary feelings adults would often label fantasy. Fantasy can play an important part in the manifestation of some desires as it creates a receptive ground for actualization. This is not to state that life is a continuous state of fantasy, but what it attempts to show is the benefits of being able to feel that which we desire before we actually have demonstrated it. This means believing in something that is more intelligent and greater than we are, something that fulfills our dreams and desires.

Note: The intelligence (Source) that motivates our desires also fulfills them.

♥

Introduction to the Three Different Levels of Comprehension

The Reactive or Physical Stage of First-Level Understanding

In this behavioristic stage the individual operates from an unexamined belief system. By unexamined we mean that the individual has never given any thought to what s/he believes is the truth. S/he has never questioned the rationality of what made up her or his particular truth. The core belief of that truth is based on facts s/he has been given by his or her parents or mentors. How and what s/he knows is what authority figures have decided for him or her. This is where the individual believes that his or her perception relates to a physical world as it is. For example, a tree is believed to be a stationary object, like a still photograph on the brain. There is no awareness that the tree is interpreted with the person's subjective reasoning. If I would ask ten people to visualize a tree, I can be certain that each person would have a different image of his or her tree. One person might have a favorite oak tree, another person might visualize a birch tree, etc. Not only will the trees differ in names and sizes but also in location and the feeling associated with the tree. We may enjoy the shade a tree provides or we may be cursing the leaves it sheds into our swimming pool during summer or autumn. In general most people are convinced and believe that they know what we are talking about since everybody knows what it means to be talking about a tree. As we gain more awareness, we realize the psychological complexity of labeling "things." In first-reality, understanding the physical world relates to the five senses, i.e., seeing, hearing, tasting, touching, and smelling.

This first-level way of thinking (not being aware of one's own psychological dynamics) is what produced the orthodoxy of every science and world religion. In different religions, the blame falls on God for not hearing a person's plea or Satan for being the powerful force that is destroying his or her livelihood. From an Eastern perspective, the individual can blame Karma or reincarnation as his or her current cause of suffering for his or her deeds that originated in other lifetimes.

Even today, American psychologists that were schooled in behaviorism do not accept the existence of internal mental processes prevailing within the individual. To the behaviorist the belief lies in the brain that is conditioned by its environment. The brain's reactions are therefore based on causes that are derived from the environment. In this level of understanding the individual is a victim of his or her environment because the circumstances have caused his or her present state of being. Individual reactions are based on a world that is objective and tangible as there is no ability to reflect on the part his or her own beliefs (habits) play in his or her reactions. This lack of awareness is what we name external or "outer" orientation where the individual reacts to stimuli believed to be caused by someone or something other than themselves.

In first-level awareness (behavioristic psychology), the individual is largely a follower and believes that s/he is a victim of his or her circumstances. This person generally follows the footsteps of his/her parents or guardians and/or follows the directions of his/her mentor(s). Although these prescribed or conditioned reactions are expressed by the individual, there is no awareness within the individual regarding a preexisting potential of change awaiting actualization. This "outer-oriented," behavioristically conditioned perception makes up the majority of the world's cultures. They work for someone else and live with the rules and regulations that have been presented to them. These people will mingle with people believing in a same or similar philosophy and most of them assume that they have no control over their situations, therefore wind up blaming the world for all their ills. In this level there is no active self, ego, or person to entertain different options for current circumstances nor is there an ability to actualize new habits.

New or better habits are taught by coaches using some form of conditioning but there is no self-realization that the potential is already within the person and does not have to be the sole work of a coach. This individual is not aware of the part s/he plays in his/her own reactions and therefore blames other people by making them scapegoats for his or her own inadequacies. The scope of their level of functioning will not extend beyond themselves as their brain is considered the director of their five senses. "It's me against the world" as there is no knowledge that a source of help exists within themselves. Life is based on factual causes that either help or hinder people's current situation or their future. Many of these people still blame Mom and Dad for their shortcomings and believe that they are powerless to make changes. Their survival is based on favorable economic trends or help from other people. Their conscious awareness is relating to a physical world producing a significant level of mass consciousness that leaves them feeling victimized by their world.

Within this group of followers, we find masters or gods promising to lead individuals to their desired goals, destiny or a place for salvation. Jim Jones is one example, leading people to mass suicide, and Hitler is another type, a dictator executing scores of people. Throughout history most cultures have been ruled by kings, emperors, or dictators. A most recent example of obeying one ruler would be the mass suicides of the Heaven's Gate people.

The philosophical system of naïve realism has taken a foothold within these people because they believe that "things" of the world are identical to thoughts perceived by the individual. This type of realism assumes that "knowing" is not part of the individual's mental processes but is a perception that is believed to be an empirical observation. In a sense this is true because without an understanding that our thoughts and our expression of those thoughts are processed subjectively (meaning that they can only be interpreted from the understanding we have), we literally believe that what we see is what everyone sees. There is no possible way to realize that judgment is based on the individual's own self-image.

To illustrate how we see, let us examine the picture created by Louis Nitti Jr.

THE OBSERVER

Of primary importance in the study of any and all ideas, is the role of the observer—you and I doing the study. Unless and until we have determined the means by which we comprehend reality—of whatever sort—there is a risk that we inadvertently omit the most important element in any study of consciousness.

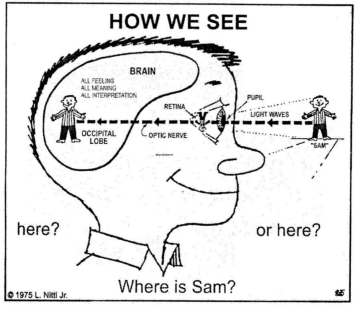

"THE LOCATION OF COMPREHENSION" cannot be overemphasized. Unless we realize the implications of this simple graphic, we insulate ourselves from the single most important factor in the understanding of consciousness. WHO IS IT THAT IS DOING THE OBSERVING? Understanding this chart allows countless problematic areas to be explained. We never do see the outside world other than in our own comprehension, fraught as it is with biases, prejudices and subjective opinion. These influences both color and determine "who" and "what" it is that we observe, evaluate and act upon.

This picture depicts how we actually see. We see Sam with our eyes, but we interpret the reality named Sam with our internal level of understanding, processing what we see externally with the help of our brain. People with first-reality understanding only relate to the Sam they see external from them. There is no realization that the process of recognizing Sam is connected to an internal evaluation. When the inner evaluation process dawns, we will have made a giant leap in the way we understand our reality.

This notion of how we "see" can be witnessed when five people observe the same accident. As the police take witness reports, they find that each person is giving them a different interpretation. How can this be when all five people saw the same accident? The answer lies in the subjectivity of comprehension the individual expresses. The way in which the accident is interpreted depends on the belief system of the individual doing the interpretation.

The same principle applies in what we consider invisible guides that are granting us answers. It is part of a faint (or sometimes not so faint) voice we perceive within us. If the answer is derived from a psychic level of consciousness involving so-called evil witches or Satan, our actions based on that level will be totally different from guides or angels (messengers) communicating from a "higher" level of consciousness. The reason we put the word higher in quotation marks is that in reality there is no higher or lower in the realm of consciousness—only different uses that correlate to each level. How they are composed or interact in actuality is part of our current research including the mystery of how these levels exist. The knowledge we have regarding consciousness is extremely limited. As we compare these levels with our understanding of kindergarten, elementary, high school, college, and post college education, we realize that a person in kindergarten would not be able to solve higher level mathematics.

In first-level comprehension, people unconsciously practice an awareness that is believed to be totally factual. The facts, however, are based on evidence that is subjectively biased even though these people believe they are relating to an external or "outer" world. (It is mom's fault, it is due to our current economy, etc.).

In our research, external or outer is considered conscious awareness of a reality that is based on meaning of an objective world that is external from the individual. It is the belief that the senses relate to the individual's environment which is the responsible cause of his/her experience. The individual's worldview is based on cultural beliefs that were handed down from generation to generation. Belief is largely accepted on the basis of authority figures deciding the meaning of truth. It is a belief that **doing** produces **being**. For example, "The harder I work the sooner I will be rich."

In first-reality, we believe that our understanding is derived from an outside world, where our meanings and feelings are the result of happenings from this outside world. (It is Henry's fault that I never . . . , or had I not been raised on a farm I could have . . .). As our understanding increases we realize this form of belief is a blind spot in our comprehension since our feelings are the sum total of our subjective interpretation. To give you an example, one hundred people can sit in the same movie theater and watch the same story on the screen. Some of these people will cry, laugh, or feel happy, or scared, while others just sit there and stare at the screen without apparent emotional reaction. Part of this difference may still be the result of our cultural upbringing where "boys don't cry" and another part has to do with the way we process information. What is funny to you may not be funny to me because our internal barometer of what we consider funny uses a different interpretation. In general, people that function more from their left brain are less likely to be emotional than people working from their right brain. Right-brain people live more in a feeling mode rather than from abstract facts. An engineer would spend most of his/her time in the left-brain hemisphere and an artist would spend most of his/her time in the right-brain hemisphere. Asking an artist to do engineering calculations would in most cases be fruitless.

When we can learn to incorporate our left with our right brain, we will be living a richer life. Both hemispheres are important and both serve vital functions in our daily lives, yet one or the other brain hemisphere usually dominates. By subjective interpretation we mean that each person interprets his or her happenings with his or her current level of awareness.

In first-reality, we chase after things as we are unaware that the desired feelings are not in things but in our "inner" awareness (unfolding consciously in second-level understanding). We often pursue people, places, and things we believe will give us the love, money, health, or security we seek. Too often, we find that as we acquire one of the "things," we again strive for the next because the thrill of getting it is no longer present. In order to keep our senses satisfied, we then have to strive for the next "thing." Things can give us a certain feeling yet this feeling is activated within the person and **not** as a result of the thing.

♥

Western Perspectives Generally Differ from Eastern Teachings

Personal achievement is viewed very differently in the West. Compared to Eastern philosophies, Western cultures stress individuation and the importance of one's environment. Awareness of individuation begins in second-level understanding in which the individual expresses as an achiever. "Doing" or achieving success has been our Western way of living where in the East "being" is believed to create the doing. Attempting to attain bliss from a strictly meditative stance is not generally accepted in the West because it ignores one's world. The orientation of individuation in the West awakens personal responsibility and the decision-making capability that has created thousands of modern conveniences and also develops a conscious awareness capability to actualize within consciousness itself.

How Orthodox Teaching Fits into First-Level Comprehension

Members of an orthodox religious group would be considered first-level human beings as their religion prescribes how they should live. Fear of eternal hell has been a giant motivator in the past and has helped to keep the masses under control. As we study ancient history, we can find the unbelievable tortures, murders, and convictions that were performed by a handful of select people who called themselves "authority." Wars are still fought today in the name of religion. As we realize that religion was often the force of political power, we can understand how such tragic situations took place because the majority of people were followers and generally less educated.

With the availability of global information we are enjoying today, we also witness many changes in beliefs, because the individual now has access to information that was previously not available or more difficult to get. With more information we notice less and less following of orthodox prescribed dogma in both secular and sacred matters, because authorities attempting to restrict freedom in living will no longer be tolerated.

For example, an Orthodox Jew has to live with over six hundred rules everyday. If you checked off every rule every day it would take you the entire day to do so. This illustration is not to show disrespect to various religions. It simply alludes to the importance of learning to question the relevance of someone else's rules.

Rather than investigating the core differences of religious practices, in the past it was much easier to forbid a person to mingle with a different faith, particularly if it meant entering into a relationship. For example, Catholics are not to marry Jews, and Mormons are not to marry Baptists, etc. Opening our scope and beginning to question our beliefs is part of a motivation that can transport us into second-level understanding, where conscious awareness deals with psychological beliefs and not with someone else's rules and regulations.

Dynamics of Change

In Holographic Psychology, differences in the way we move from one level of understanding to another level are expressed as "Dynamics of Change." As mentioned in the beginning, this change must be viewed in the context of "movement" from a present level of conscious awareness to a new or different level of conscious awareness. Processing this change involves realizing that we have something to do with the way we react and feel about any situation.

What we are experiencing is not nearly as important as what we do about what we are experiencing. One person can feel completely devastated over the breakup of a relationship and another person will mourn a reasonable time and then focus on new possibilities.

When we view life in the context of continuous change, we will have a much easier time adjusting to new or unexpected situations. Most of the population does not embrace change even if it means living a more meaningful life because the unknown can be threatening. Being attached to certain habits often creates a (false) security, forming the basis of the life we live. Unless we are open to new meanings that will increase our level of awareness, we will live our life within the boundaries that were given to us by authority figures we believed already had the truth. Questioning authority was not something we did in the past because we believed that the authority had absolute answers. Thankfully today, we have more information available than ever before in human history and we can take part in a decision that will concern the rest of our own life or the life of a family member or friend.

Just one week ago I met one of my neighbors on my daily walk. He informed me that his wife had been diagnosed with breast cancer. He stated that they had to remove one side of her breast and would then perform reconstructive surgery. My first question was if they had obtained a second opinion regarding the diagnosis and surgical invasion. The answer was no because they felt that her cancer was a hereditary factor that had afflicted her mother and other members of her family. So she went to surgery without the benefit of a second opinion and therefore will go through chemotherapy as scheduled. This couple acted on the viewpoint of their doctor (as the authority figure) without investigating different options. A second opinion may not necessarily have furnished a different approach but would have given more credibility to the given "facts."

Let me share one of my personal experiences. When my daughter was three years old, we noticed that the pupil of her left eye wandered toward her nose. My pediatrician recommended an optometrist specializing in children. I completely trusted his recommendation and my daughter received bifocal glasses which she wore for a full year until her next checkup. According to her doctor nothing had changed and the following year she entered kindergarten. When I took her for her next checkup, I was informed that her doctor was not in the office but that someone else would take care of her. First I was upset, but then I questioned his associate as to when she would be able to read without her glasses. Her response was that with this type of prescription she had never seen anyone getting out of wearing glasses. This made me very suspicious and thus I investigated and found another doctor to get a second opinion. Despite the fact that we had to wait three months for the appointment, it changed my daughter's life. We were informed that she had the wrong prescription and that she was unable to see a blackboard clearly in school with bifocal lenses. What I thought was a misfortune of missing her regular doctor turned out to be a great blessing. As we increase our knowledge, we can make better decisions.

Once we are aware of differences, we can only make suggestions to adults. We cannot force them to do anything against their better judgment. They are often unaware that their judgment is made from the knowledge they have adopted or believed and reflects their level of understanding and not necessarily the truth.

One of the hardest tasks we face is to be able to release a decision made by an individual based on his/her level of awareness. We may have two different opinions that are emerging from two different levels of awareness. Is one better than the other? No, because we can only make decisions from what is familiar and known to us. Until we begin to question our current conclusions, we can rarely arrive at a better or different decision.

Important Advice for Parents

Similar scenarios often happen between parents and children. Parents want their children to be happy and successful in their lives. The level of happiness, however, is often delineated from the view of the parent and not the child. This can bring heart-wrenching conflict as when the child refuses to follow his/her parents' advice. As parents, we are well-meaning and think that since we have more life experience we should be the ones making the decisions. Life is a school that has many lessons to teach us. We as parents do not generally know what lessons our children came to learn on this earth plane.

Lovingly releasing children to their own destiny is very difficult to our way of believing because we don't want them to have to suffer the way we did. Guiding children without forcing them to obey becomes a delicate balance that takes much courage and understanding since what we might observe is not necessarily what we would like to see unfold. Our "grand plans" have to be shelved and we have to let our children be who they are, yet support them as they are. This concept has certainly been one of the most difficult challenges for me because in the beginning detachment feels as if we are not a caring parent. Distinguishing between physical control and emotional support takes time, much patience and understanding but will be most rewarding.

The following picture attempts to give the reader an idea how we process information in first-reality understanding.

LEVEL 1

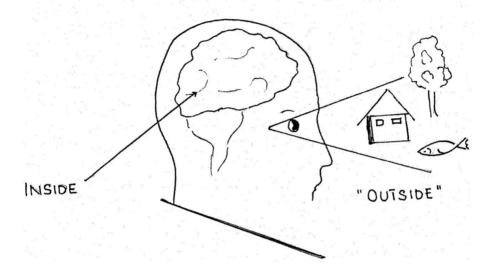

This picture shows that there is no conscious connection between an external observation and an internal interpretation.

This interpretation is based on the assumption that what we see externally is our factual reality. In truth, this external view is processed internally and is based on our current level of understanding.

The Mental or Psychological Stage of Second-Level Understanding

Second-level comprehension is the mental or psychological stage in which the human celebrates the birth of his or her awakened "self." Self is in quotation marks because we will notice in third-reality comprehension that there will no longer be a "limited self," the way we claim "self" in the beginning of second-level comprehension. An individual is able to initiate action for change because s/he has realized that s/he has something to do with the way s/he reacts to current experiences.

S/he has mastered some form of self-control through self-reflection and is now consciously aware that his or her self-image or self-esteem is based on his/her current belief system. This new focus initiates "personal responsibility" because s/he has now located where his/her psychological dynamics take place (within themselves) and is therefore capable of choosing whether to react or not react to any current experience. The person is now capable of reacting or not to his or her evaluations that formerly were believed to be verbal or physical assaults from other people. Discrimination between wanted and unwanted acceptances is based on this new reflective capability utilizing options (within one's own consciousness) rather than being a victim of old reactive habitual patterns. A realization has awakened that his/her world corresponds to his/her subjective evaluations rather than to his/her environment. This new "I" has choices available that did not exist in first-level comprehension.

Sigmund Freud opened modern psychology to the "mental" nature of human beings and the part that the unconscious plays in our behavior. Interestingly, his research was basically focused on the pathology of human nature. Freud introduced the lengthy process of psychoanalysis and many of his patients had weekly sessions for years.

When we take a look at psychoanalysis, a therapeutic process involving the subconscious, we begin to realize that psychoanalysis is still practicing first-level comprehension because even though a subconscious part of the individual is recognized, the main focus of therapy is still on the pathology or cause of the individual's reaction rather than teaching the individual how to actualize change. Psychoanalysis changes the way the individual views "cause" from his or her environment to his or her past experiences. It is not the past that needs changing or that can be changed per se. The individual has to focus on a solution orientation that is not based on a cause(s). We cannot change the past but we can change the way we view the past.

After second-level comprehension, the individual is aware that s/he is no longer a victim of his or her parents, teachers, the economy, etc. S/he realizes now that his or her prior believed victimization was due to limited subjective boundaries which s/he had accepted as reality.

This stage of awareness is the beginning of humanistic psychology and is the basis of personal empowerment. An awareness of a subjective dynamic has taken place within the individual replacing previous habits of reaction. We name this stage second level of comprehension because the individual "I" is now capable of choosing preexisting potential for implementing change. This realization does not usually eliminate all first-reality habits because one's focus may have only incorporated a limited number of second-level functioning. The person may no longer be reacting to his/her boss or his/her associates but is still reacting to his or her parents or siblings. This new realization is a process of invoking change regarding unwanted habits in areas to which we pay the most attention. With constant practice new behavior will become second nature.

This second-level realization is a total reversal from the behavioristic model expressed in first-level comprehension, for the individual is no longer a victim of his or her environment or their past. The individual is now an empowered participator forming constructive behavior as s/he practices new habits.

Changing levels in comprehension is most often a gradual process of integrating more and more areas of our life. We may first be successful using our new principles at work but may not yet be able to implement them at home or vice versa. As the quantum leap in understanding is practiced, we will witness our change in understanding bearing fruit.

To illustrate it graphically.

LEVEL 2

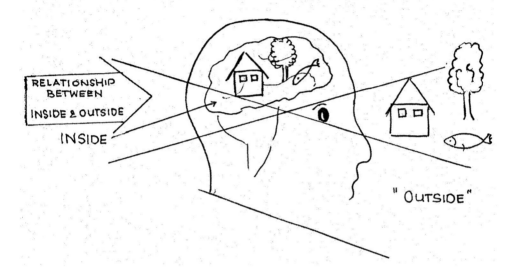

In this picture, depicting second-reality understanding, the relationship between seeing something outside and processing it as part of our internal reality is recognized.

After the individual awakens to second-reality, s/he relates to the meaning and feeling s/he is giving to his or her evaluations rather than reacting to his or her previous beliefs that were based on a physical world. The process of subjective observation (being reflective of one's experience) is realized as a function of the individual who is no longer a victim of his or her world situation. Locating where we process our psychological dynamics is what our research names "Location of Comprehension" or "Feststellung."

It represents a quantum leap in understanding. This "Feststellung" provides a freedom to consciously referee our thoughts, feelings, and actions we call options. When we act from this level of comprehension, we are aware that we are responsible for the way we feel (either good or bad). The concept is based on the understanding that one's language exposes the level the individual is currently processing. The self in Holographic Psychology is part of a preexisting wholeness, expressed multidimensionally through levels or stages of understanding, i.e., first, second, or third level. When Location of Comprehension is fully understood, it eliminates victimhood and enables the individual to choose between beneficial or harmful experiences. Mastering this theory eliminates boundaries that have been limiting human beings for centuries.

In second-level understanding, conscious awareness now deals with current psychological beliefs and the behavior these beliefs are producing. The power and intelligence for practicing change has been realized within one's own consciousness. This means that how I understand and deal with what is happening in my life is based on the level of comprehension I am currently expressing. If my views are limited, so will be my actions and my choices for changing undesirable situations. When we are capable of reflecting where we are in life, we will be able to choose different actions.

To give you one example, we can either cry or laugh over spilled beans. All of us encounter situations in which decisions or reactions are not blatantly black or white, meaning laughing or crying. We may have good reason to cry, but our daily emotions will not devastate our entire life when we have the capability to decide how long we want to suffer. In second-reality, the individual is now capable of testing his or her personal level of empowerment. What brought the person to tears in the past will now be negotiated subjectively as the capability to reflect upon one's responses is realized. If we allow someone to bring us to tears, we are operating in first-level comprehension where we are victims of our world. If, on the other hand, we realize that we are only hurting ourselves by expressing unwanted habits, we can take a different course of action by refereeing change from our initial level of emotion where we had always reacted based on our established habit patterns. We can then realize that the other person is playing his or her game from his or her perspective, based on his or her level of comprehension. How we relate will be our perspective so we stop giving attention to the perceived causal world by changing our thinking and feeling, or walking away in silence from the situation.

Nonconfrontation is extremely powerful when we learn how to implement our newfound wisdom. Mahatma Gandhi was a master at practicing this nonreactive state of being. Next time you are being stressed, try Gandhi's nonreaction. Then interact with yourself with warm loving feelings and watch what happens. Living with a second-reality understanding does not mean that the individual has to eliminate crying or any other emotion permanently, but it means that the individual now has options regarding his or her experience. In first-reality behavior, nonreaction is impossible because there is no awareness of an "I" that is capable of processing change.

Awakening to subjective orientation has multiple benefits as the individual has the opportunity to view life as a game of awakening to preexisting potential often called universal mind. Participating in our own decision-making process is empowering as it increases our own level of self-esteem. Prior to this realization, self-help systems play a major role in facilitating change. These systems can either be utilized on the basis of sacred or secular premises. As belief in the individual gets strengthened, it does not matter whether his or her practice is sacred or secular. This change is not possible, however, until the person awakens to the psychological reality that is subjective rather than objective in nature. Discovering the source of one's own evaluation enables the person to take personal responsibility for his or her actions in how they relate to their current evaluation. Discovering the subjectivity of experience and the use of language to express one's thoughts and feelings awakens conscious awareness to the existence of a preexisting potential for creating change.

Actualizing this potential opens new doorways for discovery and enhances the search for meaning. Who I am and what is my purpose in life is not a subject that would be readily discussed in first-level comprehension. Changing our own self-image changes our worldview. As we work with new understanding, we expand our boundary lines and as we expand our boundary lines we become more open and ready to accept differences.

When our self-image is exposed as our current belief system, it reveals current habits which are responsible for creating reality. A realization will take place that humans do not react to an external world (objective world) but rather to a subjective world that is based on their internal belief system. This is what our research refers to as "inner" orientation.

It is stated in the glossary yet bears repeating:

Inner: is the recognition of one's own beliefs and experiences that are subjective in nature, the individual's psychological dynamics, rather than an effect of his or her environment; a conscious identity of the self that awakens with second-level understanding; the awareness of the mental realm or consciousness that is not recognized in first-level understanding. It is a comprehension we label "Feststellung;" the realization that observes who or what is doing the observing. "Inner" is a state where *being* produces *doing*. "Inner" in third-level comprehension means being aware that a universal transcendent power is part of, and working through the individual. It is accessing the invisible powers named omnipotence, omniscience, omnipresence.

Changing from an "outer" to an "inner" orientation brings with it a paradigm shift in understanding that cannot be taught. It can only be realized and tested experientially. This increase in awareness has to take place within the individual and is an awakening of his or her mental capacities. The "I" is actualizing his or her own potential.

When we examine this paradigm shift from a metaphysical perspective, we could call this realization the science of mind. As we have mentioned before, mind does not exist consciously in a first-level comprehension because the individual believes that the meaning of anything is provided by his or her senses which is caused by his or her world or their past.

In second-reality the self-identity is born. This self, however, can still believe that it is separate from its world. Yet its new focus is now on transforming reaction toward the world with the realization of this individual power. With this awareness enters the awakening that meaning is located as acceptance within his or her own subjective belief system. When this self is born it realizes a conscious awareness that is actualizing individuation of preexisting potential as a life of empowerment and change.

With this realization comes the awareness of the subjective nature of meaning and feeling as being psychological rather than factual.

Analytic philosophy makes us aware that language is subjective and that we do not hear or see another person, place, or thing external from us. The way we hear or see our world is the result of our own evaluation, processed in our brain, with the help of our own personal biases that make up our self-image. What we see and hear in our evaluation is the sum total of the reflection of our own current understanding. This understanding can incorporate false beliefs the individual holds as true. We often witness this phenomenon with people who are schizophrenic. They can actually believe that ants are crawling on them despite the fact that no other person can see ants on their body. Part of this person's psyche has taken on a belief of crawling ants as a fact.

Plato called these internal dynamics (seeing ants) the shadows of the individual's evaluation process. They appear real but are not, once we understand that these dynamics are psychological and are located within our own consciousness. Plato's essence of life was perfect and real, but what was imperfect was the evaluation of the individual who believes that his/her evaluation is the real world. These evaluations only have permanence in consciousness for the duration of the individual's acceptance. It is further evidence reflecting our conditioned habits. Confusion can arise when we believe that what we utilize as our own consciousness is all there is of consciousness. In reality we are connected to a universal consciousness, and the part we personalize is simply a minuscule portion of the whole.

Humans must awaken to self-conscious awareness before they are even aware of the existence of their own consciousness. When this realization is perceived, we call it the "inner presence" (God) or universal consciousness.

This invisible power has always existed, whether the person was aware of it or not. Mass acceptance of this separation from the realization of constant, everlasting connection was perpetuated with the beginning of religion where God (Gods or Goddesses) was worshiped as an external creator. Therefore, the creator and the creator's creations were considered separate entities.

Good (powers that help) and evil (powers that hurt) are fictions in first-level comprehension and belong in the category of the shadows that Plato described. Within a first-level understanding, we have to have external "things" to either worship or blame as there is no awareness that the interpretation of our world is psychological and not factual.

The Key Factor to Advanced Realization

The real birth of a person is the acknowledgment of the mental aspect of a human being. His or her mind interacts with the brain creating a temporary sense of individuation. However, there is no individuation within the cosmic mind, because there is only one source of energy. Within this format, a physical object is then recognized as a psychological image that is formed by the brain/mind pertaining to a psychological evaluation of the perceived object. Feelings open our conscious awareness to concepts that happen almost instantaneously and reason, ego, self, mind (representing conscious awareness) are now capable of analyzing the experienced image within one's self as being favorable or unfavorable. A potential for change is realized. These steps are all psychological and work in concert with the individual's chemical/physiological nature learned in first-reality. In first-reality this process is viewed as a state of reaction that is conditioned by the brain. This biological orientation is not wrong but very limiting since it omits the most important ingredient namely the evaluation process within the universal mind of the individual giving reality its meaning. This evaluation process makes choosing options possible.

When we probe into the difference between an image and an object we find that an image is not a physical object in one's brain but a representation that is awaiting meaning. Meaning is realized as subjective conscious awareness that stems from an inner source that is culturally conditioned and expressed according to the particular level of comprehension. Physiological images are formed in the brain and are derived from a perceived objective world. We do not work with a physical tree in our brain but an observation and evaluation of that physical tree. When differentiation between an objective and subjective understanding is realized, it opens the self and makes possible the potential for change that can be actualized because we are then aware that it is not a physical world that is given meaning but rather a psychological evaluation that takes place within the individual.

Meaning is not only subjective within me but is also part of the collective unconsciousness that is within all existence. For this rationale to make sense we have to have an understanding that we are more than just our physical bodies. The existence of universal consciousness is validated by numbers of separate people simultaneously inventing the same item or writing the same creative data. This phenomenon explains mental telepathy. We can communicate with universal intelligence whether we are consciously aware of this connection or not. Therefore, it does not matter whether we live in the USA or the North pole.

Uncertainty Can Happen When We Move into Second-level Comprehension

Difficulties begin to arise when we move out of first-reality understanding into second-level comprehension. The outer reality of our objective first-reality world orientation begins to mix with our newly discovered inner or subjective second-reality orientation. Suddenly, confusion between the external or former truth whirl within the new found internal or subjective truth. Our new reflective capability turns into a conviction forming a new truth. Is one truth correct and the other incorrect? Who decides? Within our former belief the ruling authority has always made the decisions for us. Integrating a new level of understanding means being capable of analyzing our own sequence of reaction. With added knowledge we can now choose between the old way of recognizing and dealing with our reality that is based on our habits or choosing to implement our new formed wisdom which is capable of realizing that any reaction originates from our beliefs we treasured for so long. When this individual is capable of relating to this new reality s/he changes his/her identity and therefore his/her Weltanschauung (worldview). Choosing to react or not react is empowering because we now have newfound options available for testing a healthier state of mind we never knew before.

Recognizing this new level of awareness can feel like arrival, Nirvana, or heaven when compared to our former level of understanding but it is simply an additional step in the continuum that is part of our evolution process.

We often intellectually understand the psychological principles involved long before we integrate them experimentally. Reading about change and actually practicing change bring very different results. Reading about golf does not lead to eagle shots. We have to spend time on the golf course practicing eagle shots. Despite the fact that we are intellectually aware, we may practice this awareness in one area of our life and not in another area. We may think, act, and feel rich and actually manifest money, but in the department of our relationships we may still practice our old habits. Changing our habitual patterns is hard work. Implementing a healthy diet and sticking to it is much more difficult than riding on the roller coaster of up and down weight. So it is when we consciously begin to integrate our newfound wisdom. It takes enormous practice and an unfailing commitment to be aware of how and what we think and feel at all times.

One of the biggest misconceptions is when an individual will say or think negative things or makes judgments against another person, place, or things and then laughs it off as if it were simply a joke that had nothing to do with him or her. Unless the person understands his or her psychological functioning, s/he will not realize that these thoughts or words are actually hurting him or herself as universal laws do not differentiate between the person thinking/saying it and the person for which these remarks were meant.

Words are powerful and whether we think them or say them out loud they do affect our ways of being.

Until a human awakens to his/her "inner" side of nature, s/he cannot realize that his/her meaning and feeling forms his/her reality. This reality is made from his/her own psychological habits and not from his/her so-called physical observations about person place or thing. A basis of first-level innocence (ignorance) is when one blames unwanted situations on others when it is really a lack of awareness on how we function within our own consciousness. In time, when practicing advanced levels of awareness, we will find ourselves laughing over the naive understanding of first-level comprehension. As of this date, there is only a very small percentage of people that are capable of understanding the true functions of a universal consciousness that is tirelessly interacting within human understanding.

Changing from being a separate person expressing an external, reactive source belief to accepting an internal evaluation takes reflection, an increased level of awareness, and a commitment to test new understanding that we are all part of a universal intelligence that is much greater than our own current knowledge.

In the West, second-reality or self-conscious awareness awakens first to separate self-actualizing, individual potential before the universal Source is discovered. This individuation is part of the personal achievement of the individual. It is the process of evaluation happening within second-level comprehension of his/her awakening universal consciousness.

The notion that I create my world has merits within the self-help system experienced in second-level comprehension and has changed countless lives. Practicing daily a positive statement can certainly bring positive changes. By redirecting our beliefs and our feelings, we can enjoy enormous changes. As we advance in understanding, the results of these changes can be confusing when we created them with an understanding that is still limited in scope. This limitation has to do with the belief that we ourselves are the source of all change. We cannot overemphasize that we are not our own Source as we so often believed in early second-level comprehension. We are part of the universal Source that individualizes as our own identity. As we take responsibility for this individualized identity, our focus of attention and conviction changes. Our focus that "I create my world" still has meaning but is viewed differently with the awakening of third-reality understanding. There the individual "I" is recognized as part of the collective "I." More about the collective "I" when we examine the principles of third-level comprehension.

In second-reality we begin to celebrate an emancipation from the burdens we may have accepted about original sin, damnation, hell, or lost souls needing to be saved. We begin to realize that the language we learned was based on a symbolic interpretation rather than on truth. Belief systems operate on universal laws and correspond to the level of understanding. When we have no concept of universal wisdom, we have to have (limiting) symbols. Such symbols as Satan, (damnation), hell, etc., were largely interpreted by the ruling authorities and aided in the management of the masses. Fear is truly a potent motivator.

Heaven or hell is a concept that is created within our own psyche and can manifest accordingly. If we live in constant fear of Satan, we will attract vibrations corresponding to that level of consciousness. If we believe in God the savior and grantor of our wishes and live in harmony and peace, we will actualize a different more peaceful life. Despite the limited understanding (not being aware of our transcendent nature), we will physically practice that which is beneficial rather than detrimental.

Judgment in second-reality is replaced with a reflective capability that is observing and deciding between wanted and unwanted feelings. Old habits will be replaced with new understanding, and the notion of cause and effect will reveal itself as acceptance by degree.

When we practice positive thinking and feeling, we get positive results and the same is true for the opposite.

Jesus proclaimed it long ago, "Know ye not that ye are the temple of God and that the Spirit of God dwelleth in you? (1 Cor. 3:16, King James Bible)."

Making this knowledge available to the general population will change human society in time as the individual will realize the importance universal mind plays. When Location of Comprehension becomes apparent, universal laws will be understood as subjective dynamics residing within the individual. The former hierarchical structure will crumble and with it the "master and slave" paradigm. The student will awaken to his or her inner Source and will stop reacting to a first-reality belief where his or her environment was believed to be the cause of his or her frustrations. Reaction in second level is based on his/her own belief, and this belief exposes his or her current self-image. One of the greatest benefits emerging with second-reality understanding is that the individual can eliminate anger, frustration, excessive stress, war, arguments, etc., because s/he has now located where, why and how these emotions originate.

This realization is not part of first-level understanding because their world is still caused by their environment rather than an evaluation within their own psychological dynamics. As we implement second-reality functioning, we can celebrate the birth of what is called ego, self, or person. We have located where our emotions are expressed and have gained a new level of control. Actualizing preexisting potential is motivated from within the individual and is accessing the transcendent nature of each individual. What a change, what a challenge, as we begin to tap our own resources rather than looking for some master to do it for us.

Theoretically, we can divide second-level comprehension into two subcategories. One is the **beginning stage of second-reality** awakening where the individual becomes aware that s/he is capable of being a decision maker. It is the awakening of the personal "I" that has something to do with the way s/he thinks and feels. Self-help systems belong in this first subcategory as they encourage the individual to change by replacing negative feelings with positive ones. The other is **advanced second-level** functioning where the individual begins realizing the transcendent nature of consciousness. In order to move into third-level comprehension, the individual needs to be aware and experience their transcendent nature that exists within individual consciousness yet is an extension of universal consciousness.

♥

The Transpersonal or Spiritual Stage of Third-level Understanding

When we enter the transpersonal stage, we have advanced to a level of awareness that includes not only the objective world but also the individual's consciousness that is part of the collective consciousness. This consciousness extends beyond the person and ends the belief in separation between the person and his/her environment. This "stage" (as it is no longer an individual "I") is capable of recognizing their world as a feedback loop of the conscious level of awareness being practiced.

It still includes the awareness of one's own existence, the function of the mind, the person's own psychological dynamics, but the transcendent aspect now awakens the capability to evaluate what Carl Jung named the "collective unconscious." It is the spiritual preexisting potential that opens humans to their multidimensional nature. The immanent nature of universal mind that is realized in advanced second level is now fully understood as the transcendent level or universal consciousness.

From this third level of comprehension we understand first-and second-level reasoning, but from a first-level reasoning we would not be aware nor understand either second or third-level functioning because in the behavioristic psychology model there is no awareness of a consciousness connection, only a belief in a body with a brain that has "C-fibers" firing.

♥

In order to bring more practical understanding to the reader, we will now incorporate an example of two people experiencing the same scenario in the three different levels of comprehension. The reader can notice that even though the circumstances will be the same, interpretation will expose the different levels of understanding.

John or Mary (fictitious names) have problems in their relationship and see the cause or fault of their unhappiness within their partner or another person. If only John could be more caring and helpful, and if only Mary could have more enthusiasm for John's sport fanaticism. The lack of harmony is believed to be caused by someone or something that is "outside" the individual's awareness and understanding. In this first level of comprehension, there is no awareness that a mental functioning is taking place that is based on each individual's current habit patterns.

Looking at John and Mary's Relationship from Three Different Perspectives

Mary and John met each other during a local Christmas party, and after one year of dating, they decided to get married. They have been married for three years, and their relationship has experienced rocky periods because both Mary and John complained that each is simply no longer the person they thought they married.

John has an aloof character, is a blue-collar worker, always busy at work, and is an avid sports fan. John is happy when he can watch a game on TV, whether the lawn needs to be mowed or not. Sports come first, and if there is any time left, he will attempt to comply with Mary's to-do list.

Mary is an accountant, likes everything very tidy, and gets intensely upset when John throws his dirty clothes on the floor. She complains bitterly about John's insensitive character and states that he watches entirely too many sports programs on television instead of doing the many jobs she would like him to complete.

The conversation is as follows:

Mary: John, you make me so angry because you always just throw your dirty clothes on the floor. You watch entirely too many sports programs. There are other things in life, and you always consider me last in your line of preferences. You don't respect me, and you are just like your father. I should have known better, but when we dated, you were different; you were doing things with me. Now it appears that you don't give a hoot about me.

John: You always make a mountain out of a molehill. I work hard all day, so I deserve watching sports. It is not my fault that you don't like sports. You can do something else. Get off my back or I will just go over to Paul's house and watch the programs there. You are so nitpicky, and if you just loosened up a bit, you might enjoy sports too. I married you because I loved your sweetness. Now you are constantly complaining. Find a hobby for yourself.

Let us examine Mary and John's "scenario" from three different levels of understanding.

First-reality Awareness

From a first level of understanding, Mary sees John as a separate (external) being who is causing her grief because he does not respect her and he is sloppy. Mary does not realize that she has something to do with the way she reacts to John's accusations. Mary is reacting to his not being sensitive, being sloppy, and watching too much television.

John sees Mary as a separate (external) being who causes him frustration with her tidiness, her lack of appreciating sports, and her not respecting his hard work.

We could go on with many details, but for now let us assume that both John and Mary see their causes for unhappiness in the other partner. Neither Mary nor John are aware of the part they are playing within their own psychological dynamics, which means being responsible for their own unhappiness. Their behavior, namely blaming the other person, is what we call first-reality comprehension, and this awareness is based on an "outer" level of understanding. The object of the blame is separate and external from the person that is doing the blaming, and there is no realization that each person could choose options that would allow them to react differently. Mary is the cause of John's unhappiness, and John is the cause of Mary's unhappiness. When each partner blames the other, we have an unending cycle of blame that is based on what someone else did or did not do. Most of the population today is still reacting according to this level of understanding. This first level of reaction produces a person who believes s/he is victimized by his or her partner.

Second-level Perspective

John and Mary still have the same situation, but John and Mary now realize that the way they are reacting has something to do with their own understanding that is part of their own internal dynamics. From this insight they have a choice to either react or not react to their current feelings. They have become aware that their reaction toward the other person is within their own understanding and has nothing to do with the objective facts that were believed to be external in first-level comprehension. From a second-level comprehension, he or she can't make me angry anymore because I can only make myself angry. Reaction to angry feelings can now be replaced with something that is more pleasant. This "more pleasant" can be a positive thought or a realization of the potential for either a positive or negative outcome of their thoughts. Anger is realized as a feeling that is activated within oneself. John and Mary can still voice their disapprovals or disappointments; however, blaming the other person no longer works because they have located where and how they get angry. They both can engage in a more civil conversation and, hopefully, come up with some compromise. Both realize that they have choices in the way they react and that this reaction is part of who they learned to be (their habits), having nothing to do with the other person.

In this second-level understanding, we now have a realization that a particular reaction (getting angry) is the result of our personal interpretation (we pull our own strings) that is based on our own level of awareness and reflection. The difference between a first-level reaction and a second-level reaction is in the individual's own comprehension. In first level, we have a reaction that is pointed (externally) at the observable behavior expressed by John and Mary. The true cause for their reaction is believed to be the other partner based on what they said, did, or did not do. From a second-level understanding, we stop blaming the other person because we realize that the interpretation of their words or behavior is an evaluation that is located **within me** and has **nothing to do with the way others act and react.**

In second-level awareness, we learn to referee our own feelings. We make a decision whether we want to react negatively or positively to any situation. We feel empowered because the other person(s) no longer has power over us. We have options available to us, and we can choose whether we want an unhappy outcome or a satisfactory outcome. We have now located where the source of our anger comes from, and we can do something about it. In first level, we believed that we were the victim of the unthoughtfulness of the other person(s). In second level, we make our own happiness and other people and circumstances can no longer make us angry or unhappy. Changing our behavior by not reacting to our former habit pattern takes awareness and commitment. In the beginning of this newfound awareness, the conscious act of having to make a choice between reacting to anger or not reacting catches us often by surprise because we tend to follow our old habit patterns (automatic reaction to "external" disturbances). Being aware means that we can decide which feeling we want to animate. This does not mean that we have to simply overlook undesirable circumstances but what it points to is that we converse with the other person(s) without feeling upset. Negotiating a desirable solution has greater success when we are not vulnerable to other peoples' "verbal attacks."

Third-level Comprehension

From a third-level comprehension, John and Mary have a broader perspective giving them an overview, i.e., they have become their own CEOs. They realize that the different dynamics taking place are dependent on their level of awareness. They are choosing whether to feel victimized or empowered. From a third-level understanding, they comprehend that they are never separate from the collective consciousness (the essence of everything and everyone), and consequently they no longer will be a victim of the dynamics that can destroy or improve their relationships and therefore their lives. Mary and John realize that they are part of the same universal consciousness. When they don't react, they are able to communicate rationally and express desired emotions. Recognizing this sense of wholeness eliminates individual squabbles because they are now aware that what they think and feel originates within themselves. Why would they become angry if they are cognizant that it produces anger in them and all around them? It would no longer make sense. This realization takes awareness and practice. It means no longer reacting to other people, things, and/or circumstances. Each person has potential, and this potential either is utilized or remains asleep. If dormant, the person may never react differently. If the inherent potential is aroused, the individual will have a different life. There is no arriving because in the realm of universal consciousness, everything preexists in potential, and there is no limit to a person's actualization capability. We have just barely begun to scratch the surface of these endless cosmic possibilities.

♥

From a third-level comprehension, we realize that wholeness is the base of our existence from which we cannot be separated. So-called God-consciousness is available to every human being; however, the motivation for realization has to be present and practiced, or there will be no changes in our behavior. If we are not motivated to change, we will act and react the way we always have. Taking responsibility for our actions by deciding if we want to continue or change our experience takes questioning our current modes of thinking and feeling. In third-reality, truth is something we discover within ourselves and is not something we get from something or someone else.

What a great treasure trove! Understanding this third-level principle has the potential for total world peace because we realize that we are not separate from the Source that is creative and is part of us. Think about it. From a third-level understanding, life is a game that is predestined to express our blueprints, and this "higher power" is also the basis in our drive for actualization. From this level, we understand that there is a universal guiding principle (beyond our physical senses) that is active and is infinitely more intelligent than we are as individual human beings. Being guided means being tuned into this potential, and where this guidance will take us becomes an adventure.

Third-level thinking and acting forces are getting stronger all the time. Life can be fantastic every day instead of humdrum or unfair. Fairness validates our current evaluation when we understand the universal principles. Nobody is forced to change his/her life, and every level has its own manifestations that are based on the individual's level of understanding.

Life is indeed a school and its lessons are unending. How could we ever say that we know everything there is to know? It is simply impossible. Living with more awareness increases not only the individual's quality of life but also creates a winning situation for all. The more awareness we have, the more we enjoy our living. When we include others, we give more; when we give more, we get more. It is really that simple: when we **know** differently, we **do** differently.

The transpersonal or spiritual stage is called the birth of the infinite and includes the cosmic principles in which all life, all activity, and all existence is consciously connected as one unified ground of being. Genius and creative humans have always been channeling preexisting potential. We begin to realize that there is an inherent potential awaiting expression within every human being. From this level of comprehension, achievement is a psychological process that is the actualization of this universal preexisting potential.

With the understanding of third-reality comes the realization of an interconnection between the inner and outer that is located in a unified ground of being, i.e., this within or inner is realized as a collective expression and not as a separate personal expression.

What some people label the Akashic records is a level of conscious awareness expressing the preexisting potential that is available to everyone. All knowledge is potentially available, but we have to be familiar with the password to retrieve it in the level of consciousness in which it is available, i.e., the transcendent.

Is it for everyone? The answer is yes! It is available to everyone. We have to awaken to universal consciousness that is available right now within human consciousness, and the degree to which we are capable of awakening lies in our spiritual DNA blueprint. When numerous people tap into these "higher" levels of consciousness, everyone wins.

To illustrate it graphically:

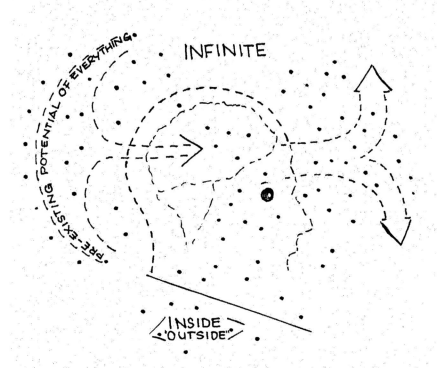

There is no separation between the inner and outer dynamics.

This third level is where religion and science merge. The beyond is realized as the preexisting potential that includes every possibility governed by universal law. "I AM that I AM" finally makes sense to me as I am included in the totality of all there is. What an awesome discovery; what a wonderful life.

The understanding of this knowledge has to awaken within the person before it can make any sense. It is not something that we can read or download from the Internet; it is something that has to unfold within consciousness that expresses as that person.

A person's reality is based on his/her current belief system or self-image, reflecting his/her current level of understanding. Change is now a process of an individual that is capable of observing where meaning and feeling actually are taking place. This inner awakening is the fundamental basis of the theory that the observer and the observed cannot be separated in one's comprehension (consciousness), only in use of language to evaluate one's comprehension.

Universal knowledge is part of an invisible, all-knowing, preexisting potential that changes the way we view and live our life, ultimately determining the quality of our life.

How This "I" of Third-reality Is All-encompassing

In third-reality, the universal Self of Western civilization (the West names God) is identical to Brahman, the Buddha, or Tao of Eastern teachings. It is the comprehension of an unlimited or infinite Source, discoverable within every human.

God is no longer a noun but is also a verb. We no longer "see" God as a separated figure, but realize that we are part of a Godhead from which we are inseparable. We are never expressing all of God, but we use the same universal mind or consciousness.

Religious dogmas fostering external deities will be superseded when we understand that spirituality or consciousness is the foundation of everyone and everything. What is labeled physical matter is viewed as an extension and a manifestation that originated in universal consciousness. The objective reality of first-level comprehension now includes a subjective understanding in which consciousness is the unified ground of being.

Creation is a process of understanding multiple levels of consciousness, and this creation is comprehended as a psychological function that uses our brain to express on the physical level. Mind and/or soul is the medium for connecting with universal mind or collective consciousness and is part of a preexisting potential that is forever awakening individually. Without its own process of awakening, (we named it "spiritual DNA"), we would probably still live in the caves. Note:

Mind and soul in a first-reality comprehension are mere words, and until these words are validated by a personal experience, they serve only as definitions that were created by some authority. Until Location of Comprehension dawns, mind and soul are not vehicles for personal use.

Third-level conscious awareness no longer separates the transcendent from the immanent. Yes, every human is part of God because all creation is God, but no human conscious awareness is all of God. Ernest Holmes stated this distinction clearly, "All ice is water but not all water is ice." In human terms, our reality is part of God, the One, Self, or Source, but not all of God. The creator and the creation express an eternal nature that emanates from the unified ground of being or universal consciousness.

In third-level comprehension, the three realities of Holographic Psychology are now understood as one reality expressing in multiple levels of awareness. The science of spirit is born and is ending the struggle or innocence we unknowingly experienced in level one or two.

The immanent and the transcendent are part of the human's conscious awareness, and God and the Self are no longer worshipped but joyfully actualized.

In third-level comprehension, Holographic Psychology is recognized as practical mysticism, part of a dynamic of an "inner," infinite, eternal energy, and an intelligence that actualizes its preexisting potential as creation.

Let Us Examine Some of the Benefits We Derive from Living in a Third-reality Awareness:

1. We move from an authority dominance to a discovery that we already have all the gifts awaiting actualization within us as preexisting potential.
2. We move from believing that God is a figure that is external from us to realizing that God is the sum total of everything. We cannot be separated from God or universal consciousness as we are part of its nature.
3. We move from surrendering to an authority to practicing refereeing desirable experiences we want in our life and stop experiencing what we don't want.
4. We move from thinking that we will experience salvation later in a "heaven" to practicing enlightenment right now right here on earth.
5. We move from looking at what is not right within us, i.e., we stop working with a pathological model and utilize our innate potential. This potential exists silently within us and beckons to be awakened. It is part of our spiritual DNA with which we entered this earth plane. Instead of working on cause, we work on solutions.
6. We move from believing that we are born as sinners to an understanding that we were simply not aware (ignorance not

fault) of the spiritual psychological dynamics governing our lives.

7. We move from believing in Karma or sin to consciously changing our unwanted habits into beneficial solutions. Working with the notion of past lives will be eliminated as our understanding no longer incorporates a so-called past or so-called future. Eternity is right now, meaning unlimited potential awaiting actualization. With greater awareness we will realize that it is not the individual that incarnates but rather an awakening universal consciousness.

8. We move from believing that "I am a limited person, I am weak, I am not intelligent, I am not pretty, into I am an individual who has no boundaries except the ones I impose on myself as beliefs and not as facts."

9. We move from a strict behaviorist cause and effect (she caused me to be angry, he caused me to lose my job) to a realization that I have everything to do with the way I feel. I am able to actualize a preexisting potential, which means that I can practice that which I want before I manifest it. Thus, reaction to an external or outer orientation changes to an inner orientation that is beneficial to my health and well-being. We name this process "acceptance by degree".

10. We begin to live life with an attitude of gratitude.

11. We move from a dualistic worldview (cause and effect of an outer orientation) to a monistic worldview, realizing that there is no separation between inner and outer orientation in conscious awareness.

12. We move from a physical-only world orientation to a physical, mental, and spiritual inclusion. We are not simply physical beings but also mental and spiritual beings.

13. We move from a world believing that our senses give us total information to a realization that our world is interpreted by our own psychological evaluations. We can only interpret anything with the intelligence we are currently practicing, i.e., level one, two, or three. Learning is no longer solely from outside sources but an awakening of a preexisting potential within all creation.

14. We move from believing that there are random selections and chance to a realization that there are absolute patterns and laws governing everything.

♥

Let Us Examine Two Major Ways for Practicing Transcendence

1. By replacing old habit patterns with new more beneficial ones, i.e., instead of reacting to mother, the boss, the economy, we realize that the reaction is a process that is activated within us and has nothing to do with other people, places, or things. We can either practice deep breathing or change the focus of attention to something that elicits positive experiences. Rather than blaming others, we will focus on positive feelings. For example, one can state out loud or silently: "I love myself. I practice peace and harmony within myself and see peace and harmony in the world. I feel happy, my daily interactions are positive, I enjoy total health, etc." Or you can reconnect with a past memory that was especially pleasant. Should you not have any pleasant memories, you can invent one since the subconscious cannot differentiate from a real and an imagined

experience. The imagined experience becomes real as it is practiced.

2. By testing the preexisting potential within myself through actualization, I begin to practice that which I want in my life rather than that which I don't want. This concept is only rational when we have at least a second-level comprehension. It is possible that before we awaken to third-reality comprehension, we may believe that we ourselves are the source of this happening. Self-consciousness is part of our finite self where universal consciousness or Self is immanent but also transcends the human consciousness. I am conscious awareness (self) within the cosmic Source (Self) or universal consciousness.

   It sounds difficult to understand, but once we realize this difference, it will solve much of the confusion that exists between Eastern and Western approaches to enlightenment. Very simply stated again, I am one part of an unlimited potential, but I am never all of the universal potential. Although I can have a greater awareness and claim several aspects of universal consciousness, I am a human conscious awareness and never all of universal consciousness. A human can express a greater awareness, and this greater awareness appears as if this person is luckier. Explaining this concept in finite terms is not possible as linear explanations are concepts of a limited conscious awareness (first-level comprehension) based on concrete objects rather than principles of unrealized potential.

Throughout history, these "higher" states of consciousness were explained in ancient myths and labeled God or Self (as the absolute). For example, the idea of God being both immanent and transcendent is very simply stated by St. Augustine in his book *Confessions,* "But Thou went more inward to me than my most inward part, and higher than my highest."

God's immanence is also expressed beautifully by Erigena, the ninth-century Scottish mystic who said, "Every visible and invisible creature is a theophany (manifestation) or appearance of God." Nothing could be more convincing than Jesus' words in John 14:20, "At that day ye shall know that I am in my Father, and ye in me, and I in you."

We can now recognize that the great founders of world religions always taught principles based on universal wisdom or third-reality comprehension. Differences in the way these universal principles were interpreted arose from the level of comprehension with which the so-called authorities developed theologies. Interpreting monistic principles into a dualistic language model is what created enormous differences in expressing truth. Without the awareness of third-level comprehension, it is virtually impossible to do justice to these principles. How can we explain something of which we are not aware?

The essence of Holographic Psychology shows the different stages capable of being expressed by an awakening human being. All human stages are based on the transcendent whole or cosmic mind, whether the person is aware of this fact or not. This is why we state that the essence of Holographic Psychology bears similarities with the hologram in that the person cannot be separated from his or her preexisting wholeness. Preexisting wholeness of universal laws are expressed as innate patterns within all of creation.

What we call the future is the transcendence or unrealized potential and is all part of the unity of religious or philosophical tradition that has existed since "time" (creation) began. Practical mysticism is expressed in the dynamics of consciousness (that which we call Holographic Psychology), exposing a new worldview. Just as biology advanced with the discovery of DNA, our research is discovering similar patterns in the cosmic or spiritual DNA, part of the psychological makeup of the human being encoded as archetypes promoting actualization. This concept is also known as perennial philosophy.

As our culturally determined psychological boundaries crumble, exploring the "inner-space" itself exposes multiple dimensions of consciousness that can be experienced and subsequently become knowable. Religious experiences, either past or present, have always helped humans regardless of their level of expression because the preexisting potential for wholeness has never been absent. Jesus used the word "faith" for humans to accept their wholeness.

Eventually, everyone on planet earth will realize the "Kingdom Within" when the individual is motivated to actualize. Believing in separate expressions is no longer valid when we discover that we are all part of an "inner" consciousness that is infinite in nature. Mystical experiences transcend time, culture, religion, geography, gender, and age.

Using a metaphor to describe a greater level of awareness, we could state that discovering or awakening to the "light" within ourselves is like moving from a room that is lighted with a 25-watt lightbulb to a room lighted with a 200-watt lightbulb. We can definitely "see" further and more clearly with a 200 watt lightbulb.

The light comparison is a simile for an awakening that happens within the individual and is not a mere reference for an objective observation. We believe that there are no limits to how far we can go experiencing the divinity of all existence. Imagine functioning on a 3,000-watt level.

With this example, we can also notice that what most of us believed to be a final truth is actually a process to be continually discovered ad infinitum. As we work on gaining greater understanding, we will discover eternal principles that take us beyond our final physical goals. Remember that Jesus said, "Seek and you shall find. Knock and it shall be opened to you." Seeking is not final but leads to more seeking, enabling us to function with a greater understanding. The search can entail spontaneous discoveries or be part of a deliberate effort to make choices. Our increase in knowledge benefits ourselves and our world. The more we are aware, the more the world around us will benefit.

Within each of us is an infinite treasure chest waiting to be opened and explored. Experiencing life is far superior to reading about someone else's life. Biographies of successful people are important and can reflect life experiences in action rather than inaction, but are not a substitute for the importance of practicing our own successful experiences. The process of living a loving and successful life entails learning to express that which already exists in potential. Living fully is not merely an intellectual exercise. It requires that we experience change within our own belief system. The individual's level of understanding determines his or her capacity for practicing this change.

As we travel this journey called life, it requires dedication and work to advance our understanding. Illumination, like achievement, is usually realized after long and constant preparation. Most of us crave instant transformations because we do not realize that life is an ongoing process of actualizing potential (enjoying the journey).

What Is Labeled Mysticism Is Third-level Comprehension

Mysticism is the awareness (consciously or unconsciously) of the transcendent nature, often expressed as "higher consciousness." Mysticism or cosmic consciousness is the awareness of the supreme identity awakened within an individual's conscious awareness in the depth of human selfhood. It represents a direct connection with a "higher" transcendent reality.

It became known through legends as gods or goddesses of ancient times related in story form. The so-called enlightened few people that were aware of their transcendent natures were perceived by the general public as geniuses. They often expressed greatness only in some area of their lives. Amadeus Mozart, for example, was a genius in music, but his life in other areas was not ruled by principles of genius or even common sense.

The twenty-first century will bring the mystical awareness of the immanent and the transcendent into human conscious awareness around the world. God or the Self will no longer be worshiped as external entities but will joyfully be actualized by humans that are awakening to their new identity. Most humans will have the capacity to govern their lives as they realize that their conscious awareness is psychological (subjective rather than strictly objective) in nature. Additionally, humans have the ability to explore and experience the transcendent existing beyond their physical bodies. Realizing and implementing this preexisting potential is what transforms human existence into a new breed of people who are capable of changing the world.

Practicing mysticism is like practicing a desired goal before we have achieved it. Feeling as if this goal has already been achieved will activate the preexisting potential into manifestation. Knowledge will be gathered from the universal Source within consciousness rather than a believed assimilation that is based on authorities-or textbook-only learning.

Why would this be so?

Because the answers are already within us.

The realization that we already hold the answers within us will change the way we acquire knowledge. One of the biggest blessings will be the capability to utilize this enormous "bank" of wisdom. Everything that will be invented in our so-called future exists already in potential within you and me.

To give you one earthly example of the process, we may know that the coat of a sheep produces wool, but unless we treat and prepare this wool and then spin and knit it, we will never get a sweater or blanket out of it. We also need knitting needles and the ability to knit. The potential for a sweater already existed in consciousness, and accessing this potential is what produced the knitting needles to create the final garment. The motivation to knit the garment resulted in the invention of the knitting needles. This motivation is part of the creative process of our preexisting potential and is what prompted tools to create the products. So it is with every invention. Connecting with the different levels of consciousness is what creates masterpieces or new inventions. Therefore, creative links wind up as innovative ideas awaiting actualization within every human being.

The potential aspect of human nature was not tackled by science until the late twentieth century. Differences in the way people relate to their world and themselves are the result of a human consciously comprehending his or her own level of understanding.

Let us quickly *review how we observe the world and how we evaluate what we see* from these three different perspectives.

Each one requires a paradigm shift in understanding before it can be experienced.

From a **first**-reality understanding, we "see" and observe an objective world believed to be factual. We live within a dualistic language system where the observer and the observed are viewed as two separate observations.

From a **second**-level comprehension, we realize that we have something to do with the way we think and feel about the world including ourselves and we have begun to understand how to participate in a life of actualization.

From a **third**-level comprehension, we have gained awareness that we are never separated from the Source of the preexisting potential that is actualized within every human being, meaning that the creator and the created are really one unified ground of being.

♥

Let Us Continue with Third-reality Principles and Examine Where Dreams Fit In

When we observe more closely, we will become aware that from this third-level awareness we can actually manifest our **dreams.** As our awareness increases, we have to be on our toes because the potential for positive experiences is equally as imminent as the potential for negative ones. The level of consciousness we tap into ultimately decides the outcome and helps us realize that we are much more than our physical body. From this third-level comprehension, we actualize the "on-goingness" of our essence. Our physical body will still die and decay in this earthly existence, yet our soul lives on. When the earthly existence stops, the transcendent existence takes over. Life is therefore also an evolutionary process of continuation.

While we are on the subject of dreams, let us take a closer look.

Our research categorizes dreams as products of different levels of consciousness. Dreams feel real at the time we enter into those levels, but we have to keep in mind that they express according to that particular level of consciousness. Tragedy can occur when the individual believes that the vivid negative occurrence s/he is currently experiencing during dream time was meant for him or her. For example, hearing voices to kill someone may never have been entertained by the individual on a conscious level, yet it can be the result of having tapped into a "lower" level of the collective consciousness. We all have the capacity to piggyback on someone else's thoughts or feelings, and we need to be careful how much power our interpretation gives to these dreams. When our perception is vulnerable to so-called "lower" vibrations, we can experience unhappy feelings that have nothing to do with us. The reason we can identify with these feelings is because we have tapped into someone else's problems or miseries. We became innocent bystanders that suddenly participated in a subconscious "show." Our subconscious awareness was eavesdropping and participating in someone else's affairs. (One of my previous clients swore that he was Jesus the Christ and came to save this world). When these subconscious affairs surface into the conscious mind, we can feel an increase in heart rate, wake up in a sweat, or feel frightened. Every thought and feeling can be an acceptance leaving a blueprint in our individual belief system.

One of the ways to handle these types of feelings is to reenter the dream state immediately and consciously change the situation or feeling (instead of experiencing a negative state of mind, we deliberately change the outcome by creating a positive conclusion). The conscious realization that we have been vulnerable to a particular level of consciousness will help ease the tension an unhappy dream may have created.

♥

It is my guess that numerous believed child abuse cases will be reevaluated in the future, particularly when there is only a statement of dream-related evidence and no physical proof. As mentioned above, during a dream state, it is indeed possible to tap into someone else's history of abuse and mistake it for his or her own. This is not to state that all abuses are not real, but in time, we will begin to recognize that experiences from other peoples' lives are possible. Realization of this feasibility will gain greater importance when the nature of consciousness is more fully comprehended.

The same principles apply for happier dreams. We can be drawn to a particular level of consciousness where "celebrations" take place with people we had never met before.

It is our belief that dreams with a particular message or prediction for the individual can happen as guidance from "higher" levels of consciousness.

♥

How Do We Perceive Ourselves?

The way we understand our self and our world has to do with the realization that we utilize mental concepts and deep-seated feelings that are based on our current psychological self-image and not on our senses. This realization presents a major breakthrough in our understanding. We act and react according to our level of comprehension and the beliefs that accompany that level. When we understand this transformational concept which is based on how we comprehend our self and our world, we have the basis of Location of Comprehension or Feststellung.

In essence, we never "see" the outside world except with our own comprehension, including our biases, prejudices, and countless other influences. These aspects color and determine "who" and "what" it is that we observe, evaluate, and act upon. It is our beliefs and the evaluation of our experiences that produce our behavior.

Why Did It Take So Long for Human Understanding to Include Conscious Awareness?

To compare, ten thousand years in human time to millions of years in geological time is like a blink of an eye. The earth is estimated to be over five billion years old. Comparing ten thousand years of human time to geological time is more interesting since the first civilization (cities and empires) appeared about seven thousand years ago.

We are told that crocodiles are over two hundred million years old. Thankfully, humans have made tremendous progress in evolution in comparison to crocodiles. Crocodiles still function in the same type of environment, have not changed much in appearance, and keep struggling for survival. In contrast, the vast majority of humans no longer live in caves and have enjoyed millions of inventions making their lives easier.

Consciousness is forever evolving, and human consciousness has to move out of a survival mode in order to advance. We believe that the process of evolution is contained within the blueprint of the universe and unfolds accordingly. As consciousness evolves, so will the human species.

A Brief Look At History
That Raises More Questions

An Examination of How Beliefs Were Expressed

Throughout history, most world religions have produced two modes for expressing their beliefs. One is **orthodoxy**, fostering the assumption that the human is an entity that is separate from God (a separate self) and this form of belief became the theistic worldview of Western civilizations which is still predominantly followed today. Theism is the belief in one God as the creator or ruler of the universe. This is where the creator and the creation are separate beings; where creation is dependent on a separate power and intelligence to bring anything into existence. This belief produced a dualistic worldview (theistic and/or polytheistic) i.e., "I am here and God is 'upstairs.'" These individuals largely believed what authorities told them. By analyzing history, we notice that theologies created a theistic model of belief, generally to foster codependency and often produce an insecure individual.

The second form of expression is contained within the practice of **mysticism**, a third-reality comprehension in which the human entity understands that s/he is no longer separate from God.

Wholeness or universal consciousness is viewed as the foundation of everything, including the human being. There is no God external from me. Jesus stated that "the Father and I are one". A realization awakens in which the individual becomes aware that his or her subjective state of mind gives meaning to their "outside" world. It is his or her thinking and feeling processes or mental state that produces the external affairs s/he finds him/herself in. Mysticism is also spiritual knowledge that was labeled "Gnosis." The word is derived from the Greek meaning a knowledge of spiritual mysteries.

We have learned that "secret organizations" such as the mystery teachings of Gnosis had testing programs in which the individual had to reveal how s/he related to his or her world. Responding with a literal-world interpretation was not sufficient to gain access to the group, but a subjective or symbolic interpretation proved an advanced level of comprehension and made entry possible. The difference in interpretation lies again between an inner and outer orientation or level-one comprehension and level two or three. Gaining access meant realizing the subjectivity of meaning and understanding of human communication in that context.

These teachings oriented the individual to his or her innate potential. Wisdom was gained through accessing inner states of being and was not credited to mentors. As stated earlier, for the Western world, it was not until the late twentieth century when humanistic psychology finally began to explore and test human potential. Prior to that time, most psychological work focused on the pathology of the individual.

As we will witness, actualizing untapped potential will create the greatest success stories in the twenty-first century. Recognizing that we have a universal mind and an individual brain is the result of awakening to a second-reality understanding. It will change the way we view the world and it will foster the inclusion of "thou," meaning the importance of others and our environment. There is still a **me**, but **thou** is now also an important part of the environment, including or mirroring our current level of understanding. The enormous interconnection of every living thing gains acceptance through greater understanding. We realize that when we help Mexico, Africa, China, or Russia, for example, we help ourselves. Global interactions have increased a thousandfold with the use of the Internet as we suddenly have instant feedback with the help of the computer, some sophisticated satellites, and fiber optics. Third-reality awakens our "spiritual Internet."

An Examination of Why These Two Different Schools (Orthodoxy and Mysticism) Can Be Confusing to the Western Seeker

The two different levels of understanding, i.e., monism (third-reality) and theism (first-reality), can bring confusion particularly to the Western seeker because in order to understand monistic principles, we have to have experienced a shift in our conscious awareness. Shifting our conscious awareness means having expanded our boundary lines and realizing that our physical existence on this earth plane is comprehended psychologically and is also linked to an eternal transcended Source.

For the Western seeker, the Self (representing universal consciousness in the East) will most likely be interpreted as an individual self (before third-level comprehension awakens spirit or soul as a subjective dynamic) because there is generally only scant familiarity with the basis of all existence called universal Self, the "I am" or the One or universal wisdom. Confusion reigns for the Western individual as Eastern teachings ask us to get rid of our ego. From Eastern beliefs, ego is being viewed as part of the individual self that needs to be outgrown (as a separate self) in order to gain Nirvana or enlightenment. With the understanding of Western third-level comprehension, we realize that our individual self is not a separate unit from the universal mind but an extension. After we become aware of the difference between the individual self and the universal Self as conscious awareness, we do not get rid of the ego because it is then viewed as an active participator responsible for decision-making capability that is connected with the universal mind. Until we awaken to these differences, much confusion will reign particularly for the Western explorer. Integrating Eastern teachings is much more beneficial when we first learn how we function psychologically, which requires studying the different psychological schools, physiology, language models, and belief systems.

Eastern Teachings Were Not Published in America until the Nineteenth Century

The difference between Eastern and Western views is extremely important. Many Eastern teachings talk about eliminating the separate self or ego without realizing the important part that conscious awareness plays in the Western decision-making process. It is not a separate self or ego that needs to be destroyed to attain enlightenment. It has to do with a self-image that is limited in understanding, needing to undergo change in awareness. This change happens when we move from a first-level understanding to a second-reality awareness. We do not have to give up desire; we simply have to realize the basis of desire. If we believe that we are limited in potential, i.e., separate from the Source (apart from God), we operate with the understanding of first-reality comprehension where we would not be aware that we work according to our belief.

For example, the more we believe that we are poor, we don't have enough, we are not lucky, etc., the more the universe will give us justification for practicing these limiting beliefs. Universal laws reflect our thinking and feeling, delivering back to us what we are currently practicing. It is stated in the King James Bible, in Matthew: 13:12:

> For whosoever hath, to him shall be given,
> and he shall have more abundance:
> but whosoever hath not, from him
> shall be taken away even that he hath.

This example represents universal laws in action and is a reference to "knowledge of the Kingdom of heaven" or preexisting potential (also called wholeness) that exists within every human being. Wholeness includes everything as potential rather than limitation.

When we view desire from a second-level comprehension, we realize that the potential for actualization already preexists and is part of our own conscious awareness desiring actualization. Being able to reflect upon these universal principles makes desire rational, producing a different way of life.

In the West, this realization (regarding a self awaiting actualization) is the birth of being able to include consciousness as the Source of our existence. This consciousness is later realized as both immanent and transcendent, including the capability to evolve eternally.

Overcoming separation from God and overcoming the belief that we enter this earth plane as sinners was the creation of politicians that developed a doctrine of codependency. The theologies became the laws of Western rulers.

Most people today no longer want to hear that they are born sinners. They want to learn how to create happier lives.

There is **no soul that is lost or needs to be saved.** The original-sin syndrome should be viewed and understood as a parable that was created to expose human awareness to the pair of opposites (good/evil, big/small). Humans don't need to be saved from hell and damnation. Humans have to wake up and become emancipated from outdated, misunderstood, and falsely interpreted beliefs. As we teach these principles to the next generation, we can create a different human being. War and hatred can be eliminated, and we can enjoy "peace on earth." Rather than utilizing this phrase (peace on earth) in Christmas songs only, we will be able to live in peace on a daily basis throughout the entire year. Consciously creating and maintaining our individual state of peace will validate a different level of consciousness. This validation is part of the testing program beginning with second-level comprehension.

In contrast, the Eastern human had to overcome Karma based on sins of previous lifetimes. Reincarnation provided a chance for improving the previously damaged self-image. Neither East nor West allowed their general population to become aware of the unlimited potential within every human being capable of being accessed during his or her lifetime.

Class societies in India still do not make this Brahman teaching available to the general public. The Brahman class uses reincarnation to keep control over the masses, the same way the Western priest class has used salvation to control the general population. As long as we believe that we are separate entities, we live in a linear, dualistic world that corresponds with that form of thinking. Therefore, we will still be unaware that our spiritual nature awaits recognition.

Exactly how this invisible body or soul intermingles with the universal consciousness is currently being researched. We do know, however, that there are levels of preexisting potential within the transcendent aspect of human consciousness.

When we understand the basis of this preexisting potential, we will see our teachers and healers in a different light. They will be the proof that the preexisting potential is awakening within ourselves. Learning is an "inner" awakening that is largely based on the motivational patterns we have been given via our spiritual DNA. Personal empowerment comes from choosing options either to react to a situation or realize that the reaction is a habit that was accepted from our parents or mentors and is not caused by input from our world. When we understand this particular, we realize that it is the awareness of the human being that changes with each paradigm shift. As mentioned before, until second-reality is integrated and practiced, the psychological nature of language remains unknown.

♥

WHEN WESTERNERS TRY TO FOLLOW EASTERN TEACHINGS

Much confusion happens when Westerners try to follow Eastern teachings because the Self, as in Eastern teachings, can easily be mistaken for the personal self. If finding the personal self were all there was in the quest for enlightenment, it would exclude the transcendent as well as the importance of others or the environment. The self can appear as a self-discovery and has many applications in self-help systems but is not a true representation of the universal Self. The Eastern searcher is trying to find the universal Self (Brahman or Atman) of a third level and does not generally work through second-level understanding. It is in second-level understanding where the individual discovers that s/he has a self, using conscious awareness that is capable of making decisions. This self means taking responsibility for our thinking, feeling, and our actions. It is part of the self-help awakening that strengthens the individual's self-image, yet it is also part of the universal Self. Eastern teachings deny a separate self and insist on one Self.

To a Westerner, finding the separate self is important as it awakens the preexisting potential which is regarded as personal achievement. An individual's achievement is not generally part of Eastern Teachings. The Western searcher for enlightenment has an added stage or step in which s/he is discovering the uniqueness of the individual (self).

Universal Source or what our organization calls third-reality comprehension is usually discovered after advanced second-level reality has been awakened and integrated. Second-reality or self-conscious awareness occurs first as a separate self actualizing individual potential before discovering that we are in fact part of the universal Source. Destiny to a Westerner includes applying originality that has been responsible for many wonderful inventions. Technological improvements have been essential in the West and part of what makes second-level functioning practical.

Individual representation and achievement have generally little meaning when regarded from Eastern perspectives as the only real purpose for living is to attain oneness or bliss. As we awaken to the psychological nature regarding our personal evaluations, we will no longer hate, be angry, hold grudges, etc., because we will have realized that we are not dealing with the other person. We are dealing with our **own** evaluation of that person. When we fully understand this principle, we will be practicing desirable experiences that benefit ourselves and the world. The discovery of the subjective nature of awareness within an individual (second-level) is the immanence or oneness of the transcendent.

Habits of mental slavery are eliminated as the individual is now in a position where s/he can referee between habits that are beneficial and habits that are no longer serving him or her. Battling two different beliefs can often create warfare within the individual's own conscious awareness. To implement new options the individual has to be dedicated to his or her new practice or the old habit patterns will take hold again and again.

Implementing new habit patterns takes enormous commitment since it is so easy to slip back into our old habits. Ask any superstar in sports or business whether or not it takes attitude and practice to win the "gold."

What the Great Teachers Were Unable to Convey to the General Public

Throughout history many cultures have declared that their teacher was a divine incarnation of the godhead. Among them are Jesus, Krishna, Zoroaster, the Buddha, Mahavira, Meher Baba, and Ramakrishna, to name a few. Each one of these great teachers attempted to help humans realize that the God they experienced was also within each person, giving them the capability of producing a life of joy and freedom. Differences in understanding are not mere intellectual discoveries. They have to be awakened, implemented, and practiced daily. Words such as spirit, soul, mind, and "inner" have been used in religion for centuries, but each person must be awakened to his/her own psychological meaning. This awakening represents a paradigm shift from perception orientation of an outer world to a conscious evaluation process that takes place psychologically within the brain/mind determining the meaning we give to our perception. The way the individual relates to his or her evaluation changes the way s/he views his or her world. Blaming someone for his or her happenings changes to self-discovery, refereeing, and the realization that all interpretation is based on the person's current level of understanding. As long as I can blame the world, I have not realized the awesome power station that exists within me, let alone how I am using this power station. Feeling empowered is part of waking up to second-level comprehension. The self-image changes from playing the victim role to taking responsibility for our thinking and feeling.

Words such as transpersonal consciousness, collective consciousness, or universal mind now relate to the transcendent nature of a human being which is realized as a preexisting potential that awaits awakening or actualization within all creation.

Interpreting the teachings of Jesus requires a third-reality comprehension because these teachings are based on preexisting wholeness. Jesus tried to awaken his followers to the divine nature that exists in each individual. "The Christ" (the anointed one), and Gautama, "The Buddha" (the enlightened one) tried to explain what happened to them after experiencing universal mind. However, the general population was not capable of understanding what these leaders tried to convey. How can we understand something we are not even aware of?

I can tell you about the wonderful state of peace and love I am able to gain during meditation but how can you relate to this feeling when it is totally foreign to your way of experiencing the world? When we understand the perfection of wholeness, judging someone will no longer be rational, because the individual is really judging himself or herself. In a third-reality understanding, the individual is no longer considered a separate island but part of an ongoing awakening Source we can name God or Self. It is no longer God and the meaning that I live on earth and God lives somewhere in heaven. It is God **as** me. Again, I am not all of God, I am made in the image of God. Universal consciousness is the foundation of all awareness.

In the King James Bible, Luke 17:20-21, it is stated:

> "And when he was demanded of the Pharisees,
> when the kingdom of God should come,
> he answered them and said, The kingdom of God
> cometh not with observation:
> Neither shall they say, lo here! or, lo there!
> for, behold, the kingdom of God is within you."

Mystics have often described these levels of God or consciousness as:

Sleeping in the minerals
Awakening in vegetation
Conscious in birds, insects, and animals
Self-conscious in humans
God conscious in mystics

Even the basic teachings of Western mystics proclaim one Source or one God. This does not make the human level of understanding equivalent to all of God, the way a first-level individual understands God. As long as there is no awareness of the transcendent nature existing within each human being, this one Source does not make any sense.

With the awakening of the transcendent side of our nature, we are no longer feeling lonely or alone as we realize our connection with everything. This is not possible in first-level understanding because we believe that we are a separate being. Being alone can indeed feel lonely if there is no awareness of our connection with the infinite.

When we realize that locating our own psychological dynamics makes conscious participation possible in "the kingdom within," we stop being victims. We practice motivation within our own consciousness that is limitless and therefore we are capable of activating change. Conscious awareness is a mental activity of consciousness and not simply sensing a physical world. In first-reality, however, it is a belief that we sense a physical world externally that many ancient sages called an illusion because they were aware that the experience was the transcendent being internally experienced.

Our perception is evaluated and is given meaning (as a psychological dynamic) which is a process within consciousness. The world is not an illusion. The illusion is created when we believe that we see the world like a photograph. If we retrace our steps to the earlier part, where we mentioned visualizing a tree, we will remember reading that each person may "see" a different tree. Without increased awareness, we can assume that we were talking about the same physical object.

When we recognize how we interpret language as a description of the world we believe in (we call it Location of Comprehension), our self-image changes because it eliminates operating within the former believed boundaries that were limiting our self-image. As long as we believe that there is only black and white we have an easier time in a sense because it eliminates dealing with all sorts of shades of gray. However, as we expand our awareness (accepting gray), we become more tolerant of other opinions, other beliefs, and habits. Change means being able to abandon our small circle and enter into a greater level of awareness. There is no limit to how far we can go. The greater our awareness expands, the more we realize how little we really know.

Individual boundary lines are not a matter of one person being right and the other person being wrong. They have to do with the way we assess our current evaluations. For example, if we live our entire life in one city, how would we be able to know what it would be like living in the adjacent city, the adjacent country, etc. The more awareness we have, the greater the options are to make decisions. When we are capable of working with numerous options, we will feel much more empowered because we reject thinking that there is only one way to solve a problem.

What Happens When We Don't Understand the Difference Between Eastern and Western Teachings?

Not understanding the differences between Eastern and Western teachings has created problems in many religions because practicing monism for the Western seeker can be viewed as blasphemous, particularly in theistic religions such as Judaism, Christianity and Islam. In theism, God is the creator (infinite) that is separate from the created (finite) world.

Great confusion exists when a theistic clergy is asked to interpret monistic writings. Humans in first-reality understanding are not aware of these differences and when attempting to translate monistic writings (with a first-level understanding) will create a different interpretation because theistic explanations are based on a dualistic model of understanding rather than monistic principles. An individual, whose beliefs are anchored in the theistic model, expresses finiteness of the human body, where in monism the conscious awareness relating to the body is viewed as immortal because the creator and creation are not separate. We can notice that it is impossible to translate a monistic model with an understanding that is based on theism. The cosmic mind is the universal mind from which the individual is not separate. This distinction is not made clear until the individual wakes up to an advanced second-level comprehension in which the nature of consciousness is understood as a psychological comprehension that is immanent and also transcendent.

The main difference between theism and monism is that theism always requires a force that is external or separate from the individual. This belief is the basis of first-reality understanding. Monism or third-level comprehension is when the individual is capable of living in a reality in which s/he is aware that s/he is no longer separate from the Source of all existence. Creativity is practiced within the individual's consciousness, yet is always connected with universal consciousness.

With third-reality comprehension, we also become aware that the present (or past) is part of eternity expressed as vertical time, meaning an eternal present. Past and future are psychologically recognized as illusions that simply fill a need for the masses, functioning within a first-reality language model, validating a worldview of space and time. There is no physical time in eternity, the way we discern and allocate it on this earth plane in first-reality. As mentioned earlier, when we speak of beginnings and endings, we operate in or from a dualistic-horizontal framework which is based on believed increments of time and space. To this day, most people are not aware that this dualistic model creates a believed separation from wholeness which is the foundation of all dualistic existence, i.e., I am here and you are there. In reality, we are functioning in an eternal existence that has no beginning and no ending. This explanation is complicated and impossible to comprehend when there is no awareness of the infinite existence of a transcendent universal consciousness from which we are never separate.

When we fully enter third-reality awareness, we begin to practice principles of divine existence on this earth plane without feeling separated from God. With third-level awareness, we experience another quantum leap in understanding that can be confusing because from that level there is no longer the believed existence of an individual "I." You may ask, how can I no longer exist? The "I" called Margrit still exists, not as an exclusive unit of consciousness but as an extension of universal consciousness. The individual is not the sum total of God but is an extension of God. This form of practice is the realization of a unified single cosmic Self from which we cannot be separated and is the essence of monism. Monism awakens the individual to the understanding that the creator and the creation are one unified being, holding a capability to discover the unlimited potential that is ever present in universal consciousness.

Confusion between a theistic model and monism has been the basis of religious wars that have raged for centuries. After we realize that our meaning is psychological (Location of Comprehension), we become aware that Judaism, Islam, and Christianity all have different names and customs for the same universal laws.

What Does It Mean to Live within the Principles of Monism?

Living within the principles of monism makes for a different life where all the previous levels of comprehension still have their rightful spaces yet are viewed inclusively rather than exclusively. In other words, there is no level of comprehension that is either removed or viewed separately from the totality of universal consciousness, wholeness of God. Judgment is abandoned and viewed simply as a level of expression that correlates with a particular level of comprehension. Judgment in second-level comprehension is understood as judgment against one's self rather than the other person, place, or thing because the individual is now aware that s/he is dealing with his or her own belief system and not with his or her world. An intellectual perception of this reality can be present long before it is capable of being fully lived. Frustrations can occur when we believe that we understand the principles but are unable to manifest desired results.

When third-reality is practiced only intellectually, we can have mood swings by dipping in and experiencing first-or second-reality reasoning. When this swing is tapping into first-reality functioning, the individual will believe that the experience is caused by someone or something that is external from him or her. This individual often becomes a victim of his or her circumstances by being unaware of his or her psychological dynamics (capability of conscious control) which is initiating change.

When tapping into an intellectual second-reality model, the individual can believe that s/he is the cause of his/her circumstances, and therefore s/he believes s/he is the responsible party for turning an unacceptable situation around. This statement is partially true but misses an important aspect. How do we recognize this aspect? When we become self-aware of how we function psychologically. It means understanding the dynamics of his or her psychological functioning where s/he becomes aware how meaning is acquired and how his or her hearing and sight behavior patterns respond to his or her world as a reflection of his or her own evaluation. This form of interpretation will bring to light how the individual's thinking process is encoded into words and decoded into his or her behavior. The reaction of this individual is based on his or her level of understanding and is expressed accordingly. To illustrate it bluntly: A person that was raised in an orthodox environment would most likely not be open to different religious views. A first-reality individual would not be aware how his or her belief system shapes his or her life. This individual would most likely not react favorably if s/he was told that there was a part within him/her that was responsible for his or her reality. To sum it up, we can only act and react with the understanding we were given by a higher intelligence (we may call it God's gift of our "spiritual DNA"), our biological DNA patterns, and additional knowledge acquired from our mentors. What becomes our cultural belief is modeled by our mentors and will be accepted until we begin to question the rationale of our acceptances.

In the past the majority of people seldom questioned what authorities told them. Thus, it is possible to understand the principles of third-reality in various areas, yet still activate unconsciously certain beliefs of second or first-reality reasoning. Living in total harmony of third-reality is what an accomplished mystic practices on a daily basis. For mortals this way of life is easier said than lived as our dualistic beliefs and habits keep fighting for survival.

What Do Boundary Lines Have to do with Religion?

One of the reasons we have few options in religion is because most orthodox religions have firmly set boundary lines. Living within these boundary lines starts to change when we begin to question the foundation and validity of any orthodox religion. If we follow their dogmas and principles without any inquiry, we will never have to deal with options because the "truth" has been established. Much of what we believe is not based on the divine truth the Buddha or Jesus taught but became theologies established by the rulers of olden days. These theologies served as psychological models sanctioned by authorities and became conditioned truth fitting first-reality comprehension. The population based its life on evaluations that were formed in first-level comprehension.

Reaction to an external world promoted the birth of many gods. Even in ancient times, people prayed to the gods of wind, water, fertilization, harvest, etc. When disaster struck it was believed that the gods were angry. Therefore, a culture obeyed their rulers by practicing rituals and sacrifices to appease the different gods.

We notice that the creation of polar differences such as good/ evil, big/little, rich/poor, sick/well, life and death created a dualistic world. Heaven and hell were earthly creations that kept the population under control. Today we understand that heaven and hell are conditions that humans create where they live. Heaven or hell is a state of mind, expressing either innocence (ignorance) or wisdom. Living in harmony, in love, and in peace is living in heaven right here on earth and living with hatred, anger, and war is living in hell right here on earth. The ruling authorities used Satan or evil for controlling the masses. Remember most people were not educated and followed the rules via their authorities. In most cases they had no other choice. If they tried to question the rulers system they were usually executed.

Let Us Take a Brief Historical Look Including How Language Was Used as a Form of Self-Expression

Before language was pictured or written (about 3000 BC), we had no actual records except for artifacts. Early civilizations like Mesopotamia, Greece, Egypt, and Rome are important because they were the first to leave written records of what and how they thought. This period signaled the beginning of conscious awareness of how humans related to themselves and to their environment.

In the prehistoric age, the Polynesian settlement of the Pacific islands kept no written records yet freely moved about this planet. They formed groups, lived with their traditions and habits, and carried no more than their tools. They had no specific ties with their current living space and did not expand their habitats like later Western civilizations.

In the West, ancient Greece and Rome kept records, produced numerous maps, and as a society expanded into different countries and cultures.

History also reveals to us that prior to the fifteenth century, the majority of the world was controlled by rulers (and still is to this day). These rulers created the orthodox religions and social systems of class hierarchies of the "haves and have-nots."

Much of the physical world was revealed to Europeans within the two and one-half or three centuries after 1492. Frenchmen in North America armed the natives against the British, and the British armed themselves against the French. French, British, Portuguese, Dutch, Spaniards, and later Germans and Americans battled against each other, attempting to conquer the world. Battles were moved by greed, by love of adventure, or by sheer desperation to defend the place they called home. Many battles were fought due to the conviction of their rulers that they were doing God's work or that they were bettering the life of the people they conquered. They forced their will and religion on weaker races. Land was taken from natives, and they were enslaved. They were forced to accept the rulers' choices, whether they were sacred or secular.

With Columbus's discovery of the New World at the end of the fifteenth century, change in personal freedom began. Comparing this time frame with the evolutionary history, we can notice that the change is only five hundred years old.

As nation fought against nation, there was no attention placed on the individual. Information was established through their religious leaders or secular rulers and varied according to culture. Salvation was part of an attainment that was achieved through their religion. Rights of the individuals were established by the rulers. Life was lived and evaluated by the five senses. The realization or importance of a self-image did not exist and was not practiced with awareness until the 1960s, a mere forty-plus years ago.

The discovery of new worlds in the fifteenth century enabled Europeans to move about for the first time in history. In the beginning of this Renaissance (1463), the Hermetica or mystery teachings from Egypt were translated for patron Cosimo de Medici by the Italian scholar Marsilio Ficino. This ancient source of wisdom proclaimed a mental nature of human beings and became available to the ruling class throughout Europe. The application of these hermetic teachings was through independent study and provided the beginning of an end to European church-dominated education.

The Upanishads, consisting of discourses on the human soul in relation to death, moral choice, destiny, and the divine nature of humans, were imported to the West around 1795. This Hindu philosophy revealed that enlightenment was possible in the current life span rather than after death. The teachings exposed immanence, an indwelling spirit within the human soul present within every human being. The creator of nature is the Source and the soul of creation. The realization of innate patterns unfolding within human nature is taking centuries to be fully comprehended.

The most momentous and far-reaching conflict of ideas within the established church occurred with the Protestant reformation. Revolt against the Catholic Church began in the sixteenth century but emerged with the leadership of a monk called Martin Luther (1483-1545). On November 1, 1517, he nailed ninety-five theses to the door of the court church at Wittenberg in the German state of Saxony. His thesis demanded change and challenged the authority of the pope in Rome, including the authority regarding priests.

Martin Luther replaced the authority that church officials enjoyed with the truth and wisdom found in the Bible. This reformation changed the focus from the power of the church and church authorities to individuals. It established the importance of a direct relationship with God without the need of any church.

The importance of the human was stressed. Active humanism started in Italy in the sixteenth century and promoted the individual to seek God within him or herself. This opened the door to science and technology as a result of self-empowerment. Many new "scientists" emerged and debated over their inventions. An orientation alluding to harmony between the cosmos and the individual emerged with the German born Johannes Kepler (1571-1630) and astronomy was changed forever. This interaction between the cosmos and humans was considered ludicrous by church authorities. Galileo, the Italian physicist and astronomer (1564-1642), was only eight years older than Kepler. His inventions forced the church to demand that Galileo recant his observations and theories or face house arrest. Inventing new principles was still dangerous when it challenged church authorities.

It was René Descartes (1596-1650) who developed a philosophy that was both rational and capable of appeasing the restless. His inquiring spirit of the time satisfied the human need for certainty by separating the human mind from the body. Descartes' teaching influenced a philosopher in the late seventeenth century. His name was Baruch Spinoza (1632-1677). He used reason and attempted to show that the mind and body were not separate.

Meanwhile in England, a new philosophy opposing the rationalists created the foundation of empiricism under the tutelage of John Locke (1632-1704) who attempted to show the limits of human knowledge. It was, however, the Scottish philosopher and historian David Hume (1711-1776) that took empiricism to a new high by proclaiming that life was totally experienced by the five senses. He advocated that there was nothing to perceive other than the physical sensations. This view is what promoted analytical philosophy in the twentieth century to proclaim that because language is subjective there can only be individual conditioning and not a physical world to which language relates. Any speculation about a physical world requires some form of validation. Hume denied that metaphysical questions can be validated, thus promoted complete skepticism except for materialistic, scientific research.

The eighteenth century brought opposition to the materialism that science was discovering. This new orientation ushered in the Romantic period where the German philosopher Georg Hegel (1770-1831) introduced the philosophy that the relationship between humans and nature was mental. This concept was known as absolute idealism which began to disregard "creeds" of the current religions and focused on the innate nature of life as potentially actualizable. Poets and transcendentalists gave voice to mystical pantheism proclaiming that the nature of God existed in both nature and humans and they created elaborate writings, reflecting this interaction between mind and body, creator and creation.

In the nineteenth century, the romanticism of Europe reached America and began in New England as transcendentalism. This philosophy fascinated many literary minds and they either adopted or rejected the idea of going beyond ordinary or common sense experience, i.e., first-reality conditioning. This unity concept contained an infinite model believed to include human consciousness. Today we can still enjoy the masterpieces of transcendentalists such as Ralph Waldo Emerson (1803-1882), the naturalist, author Henry David Thoreau (1817-1862), and poet Walt Whitman (1819-1892). They believed that human freedom and glory of aspiration came from intuition rather than reasoning. Transcendentalism created lasting masterpieces in American culture and shaped American idealism.

This idealism expressed as a self-reliant human who felt divinely guided by his or her conscience. The foundation of transcendentalism emerged from the founder Emmanuel Swedenborg (1688-1772) who integrated Hindu monistic thought with Buddhism, Taoism, the Hermetic writings, along with Kabbalistic teachings advocating healing through enlightenment, capable of being practiced by the individual.

These so-called metaphysical teachings varied in interpretation, depending on whether they were considered a division of philosophy or religion. Systems that were considered both scientific and spiritual became known as Theosophy, Spiritualism, Religious Science, Unity, and Divine Science.

In the late twentieth century, philosophers divided Existentialism and Analytical Philosophy into two schools. Existentialism is the doctrine where a human forms his or her essence of life by taking responsibility and creating personal freedom. It starts from a concrete individual experience instead of abstract theories and tends to exclude the human ability to discover the meaning or purpose of life. Analytical philosophy was largely based on the writings of Austrian Philosopher Ludwig Wittgenstein (1889-1951), and it attempted to follow the principles of the empirical sciences.

♥

By now we notice that when nation was fighting against nation and until the twentieth century, little attention was placed on the importance of the mental nature of human beings. Salvation continued to be prescribed by the rulers. Humans were believed to be finite beings; there was no self-reflective capability for the general population because most humans were too busy trying to survive. What we take for granted today such as electricity, cars, information systems, and gadgets of every kind are of recent origin.

Living, for example, without hot and cold running water would no longer be acceptable in most Western civilizations. Our technological advances have been staggering and continue to be so. We are currently at a place where we are not only capable of advancing our technological world but also the knowledge of our mental world by researching the human potential.

It might also be interesting to note:

How Religious Theories Actually Develop in the Ancient Worlds

When we move from the Stone Age history into the formation of early civilization, we become aware that our ancestors used mythological symbolism to assist them to overcome fear.

When we speak of mythology, we have to thank a prominent Swiss for clarifying secrets behind it. Carl Gustav Jung (1875-1961), one of the first major European psychiatrists and psychologists, devoted his life studying mythology. He studied Chinese, Egyptian, Greek and Roman Gods and Goddesses, African and Indian demons and divinities, totems, animism, ancient symbols, motifs, and countless mythological motives.

Working with hundreds of people, he found that these ancient mythological images appeared regularly and unmistakably in the dreams and fantasies of so-called modern Europeans despite the fact that they were never physically exposed to them. Thus he reasoned that these mythological motives must be innate images contained in the entire human race. This phenomenon is like sharing a membership in the collective unconscious transcending the person. Jung named these universal patterns "archetypes," meaning that within every human being is a mystery of transcendence or unrealized levels of consciousness acting according to its level of expression.

♥

Despite the fact that we have learned to communicate with people in many different cultures, we have not achieved peace on earth.

How Can We Achieve Peace on Earth?

We can achieve peace on earth when we realize that peace is not in one religion or another but is due to the peace we cultivate within ourselves. If we believe that others are evil, we have to fight them. Evil is ignorance but as long as we don't question our given beliefs, nothing will change. We can actually worship a rock and get results if the belief is present. Belief is not in the rock, it is in the individual.

After second-reality awakens, we realize that the principles regarding psychological dynamics do not differ. They are merely expressed differently in different cultures. A paradigm shift in understanding happens as we locate where we interpret our meanings and feelings. With this shift in understanding we no longer separate humans according to race, creed, class, nationality, sex, gender, etc., because this separation is no longer a factual description as believed in first-level comprehension. Value judgment in these categories is recognized as a form of personal bias. Predicates are no longer objects based solely on a material world but are now recognized as functions of the meaning we have ascribed to them. The evaluation is then a function of our own psychological process that is subjective in nature (We can only express with the understanding we have.)

Every human is a practicing believer who is exposing his or her current use of their transcendent nature. Being an atheist is a form of belief. It is irrelevant how a person spells his or her belief. Spelling is usually culturally determined but does not differ in its application. As modern science and religion deal with human consciousness, the differences between cultures will still be enjoyed because the underlying principle responsible for all creation is the same. It is the ignorance of our own transcendent nature that produced idols in every culture. People that awaken to their transcendent nature are often called "geniuses." Geniuses have always been the groundbreakers of change in every culture. When we begin to live a peaceful life, we will have a peaceful world.

While We Are on This Subject, Let Us Examine a Possible Cause for the Continuation of Violence

Violence is largely a result of being ignorant regarding the psychological nature of emotions and the meaning given to them. It is perpetuated primarily subconsciously because most people have no idea that what they think and feel (practice) is what they produce in the(ir) world. The more people tune into violence, the more violence they (we) will experience. This mass hypnosis creates an epidemic fever that is very contagious. We can change violence with education and by deliberately choosing and changing how we relate to our environment, but first we have to be aware of the principles that produce our environment. We are all connected in this invisible, electromagnetic field and that is the reason why one person can influence the matrix we refer to as universal consciousness.

Once we are aware of this interconnection, rather than watching or playing a violent program, we will choose a pleasant production, read an informative book or listen to enjoyable music. When we realize what produces violence in us and the world, why would we continue to foster such negative states of consciousness? As we practice any tranquil state or a form of meditation on a daily basis, our internal state changes. The more peace and happiness each individual practices, the more peace and happiness we will have on earth.

We realize that there are many facets connected to this subject and the answers are complex. However, education regarding the importance human mind plays has to be integrated early in life in order to witness beneficial changes.

Just yesterday, a television station announced on the news that the city will create a new task force that will prepare for potential terrorists. This new focal point will add many more people focusing on violence even if it is meant to prevent it. The thought of planning alone will activate that level of consciousness. During commercials they also showed previews of a new movie with multiple acts of destruction. Each person that pays to see such nonbeneficial stories contributes by generating negative vibrations in the universe. The more people connect with violence, the more these vibrations are activated.

Let me give you an example that might help explain how violence is perpetuated in the world. Imagine a plain bucket of water (as human consciousness). Each time a negative deed happens, one drop of red food coloring is added to that bucket of water from which we are all drinking. Picture if every drop of food coloring were a destructive act, how red the water would be at the end of just one day! Multiply this unconscious participation by 365 days and the world population. We would all drink from this bucket of harmful red water without being cognizant how it became so intensely colored and/or contaminated. One act of violence influences the world. One drop of red food coloring will taint the clear water because it is impossible to separate the one red drop from the rest of the water. Thus whether we practice violence or not, we will be affected not only personally but globally. The more sensitive a person is, the greater would be the influence.

Before we become aware how spiritual laws work, we unconsciously drink from multiple red solutions that are created all over the world. We can't participate in consciously changing the outcome (executed by spiritual law), until we begin to realize the role we play in such interactions. Change does not lie in the simplicity of this example but in the capacity to discern and utilize universal principles. It has to begin with a change in understanding, leading to how we function psychologically. In order to achieve global peace, this interaction needs to be taught to our children, starting before kindergarten.

Locking people up behind bars (for minor offenses) is not the answer as it won't change their way of thinking. We have to make fundamental changes in the way we understand our mental belief system which directs our physical body. When we realize that what is happening in the "outside" world is a reflection of our state of mind, we will be more careful how we think, feel, and act. The greater our level of awareness, the more we automatically include others and the less we will watch anything of a violent nature. It will no longer be me against the world it will be me as part of the world. Like the late president John Kennedy stated, "Ask not what your country can do for you; ask, rather, what you can do for your country!" When we become aware of this interaction, we will be supportive of the dynamics at work rather than sabotage them. Change has to start within each individual person. When each person "teaches" (by being an example), we will celebrate a world of cooperation instead of competition.

We can still compete in sports, etc., but the competition will no longer be to the detriment of others. Losing a game is not like losing the foundation of our existence. Respecting the laws inherent in universal consciousness will bring phenomenal changes as we learn how to demonstrate desires that are already present in potential.

♥

Questions Answered

In the beginning, we promised that we will answer many questions that have been confusing for centuries. Again, we will attempt to integrate the principles that are most important to the answers. The reader might want to be aware that anyone of these questions could lend itself to writing an entire book. For more clarification let us begin with:

What Is Subjective Comprehension?

Subjective comprehension is the level of awareness we use to make our world rational. It is based on our internal sense of meaning-making, expressing our beliefs and habits. It is a level within consciousness that in second-reality understanding becomes aware of the subjectivity of language when interpreting any person, place or situation.

It is where conscious awareness interprets data at the current level of comprehension within the individual, or the "assumed" knowledge of the individual's consciousness that in first-reality is interpreted and perceived as an objective world. The interpretation is exposing the person's reality. It is the "aha" moment when the person realizes the personal interaction demonstrating his or her internal state of mind. Knowledge of a subjective comprehension is not realized in first-level comprehension because the five senses are believed to be furnishing direct "knowledge."

For example, the definition of a chair has different interpretations. If I visualize a chair I might use the mental picture of my most comfortable lounge chair, where another person might see his office chair, her kitchen chair, his/her living room chair, etc. As we become aware that each "chair" interpretation is different despite assuming that we are all talking about the same object, we will also realize that my interpretation does not necessarily match yours. When we understand that these meaning differences are based on the subjective understanding of the interpreter, we will no longer get upset over misunderstandings, because we will have realized that it is our reality or level of comprehension that gives meaning to our world. A particular subjective understanding derives from what we have been told is true, reflecting the basis of our current level of understanding. In most cases, confusion and misunderstanding stem from opposing interpretations. A conversation between people, assuming that the other person is expressing the same level of comprehension, is what usually creates utter frustration.

We can only interpret someone or something with our own level of understanding.

The greatest awareness comes with the recognition that it is not what we see, hear, touch, smell, or taste that creates our reality but what we do psychologically with what we see, hear, touch, taste, or smell.

If we linger in negative experiences, we enhance these encounters and proliferate more negativity in ourselves and the world. Being able to change negative experiences comes with second-level comprehension where we learn to referee our experiences.

To give another example:

One of my clients states, "How can anybody be so cruel and how come they cannot respect my property?" The answer is of course that "they" do not live with the values and ethics (same level of understanding) my client does. If "they" had the same values "they" would not be cruel and would respect her property the way she respects it. On the other hand, as long as she tolerates "their" behavior, she has work to do on her own self-image. When we stop playing the victim role, the perpetrators may also change or will find other "targets/victims" to prey on.

Life is mirroring what we have to learn and it exposes the level of our own reflective state. If we are in a peaceful state of mind, our world will be peaceful; if we are in a distressed state of mind, our world will reflect distress. I am sure that each person has experienced this correlation (mostly without being aware of the corresponding laws that create it) that when they are in a good mood everything is going smoothly and when they are in a bad mood, every traffic light is red, the contract was not accepted, the client arrived late, the economy is not healthy, etc.

Manifesting a correlating outcome of our current level of thinking and feeling is often instantaneously demonstrated. Remember, it is our current evaluation that is giving our world its reality.

How Universal Law Performed in My Own Experience

During a particular event I was expressing anger, and minutes later found a parking ticket on my car. This incident intensified my angry state. My well-conditioned habits initiated instant feelings before my rational mind kicked in attempting to make the necessary changes. The parking meter had expired by one minute. This demonstration made me aware how instantaneous our current experiences can manifest as validation. Replacing angry feelings with beneficial feelings takes enormous practice because it is counter to our cultural norms. When we get sucked into a level of consciousness that is unacceptable, we have to make a decision and act quickly as these vibrations create more of the same.

Some days changing and refereeing our emotions will be fairly easy and other days the change will take immense conscious work. Mood fluctuations mean experiencing differing levels of consciousness. Once we realize, however, that we are only hurting ourselves, we can act appropriately. This realization alone will change our lives. Instead of carrying angry feelings within us, damaging our own self, we will make the necessary changes in our way of thinking and feeling to accommodate a happy existence. Anger begets more anger and layers our cells like an onion. When we have too many layers covering our cells, they will be unable to breath and the consequence will be some form of illness. Forgiving is releasing our own body from negative patterns and has nothing to do with the other person. Hate or anger only hurts ourselves.

Stop negative patterns right now and witness what happens to your state of health when you practice love, joy, and abundance.

You may wonder, if we can manifest negative experiences instantly, why would we not be able to manifest positive experiences instantly? The truth is that we actually can, once we totally accept and follow the laws governing this universe.

Most of us receive to the degree we are open to universal acceptance. We may not be aware consciously that there are universal laws mirroring our self-image. Often conditioned habits are deeply anchored in our daily expression. If, however, we fully believe that God (infinite potential) is our only Source and that we cannot be separated from that Source, we will be able to manifest instantly. If on the other hand we believe that we have to physically earn everything first, the universe will give us plenty of time and opportunity to "earn" our desired goal.

How Do We Create Change?

Experiencing earthly struggles seems to be a way in which our evolving nature forces us to become reflective and enlightened. There is a saying that without the valleys, we would not appreciate the peaks. The most profound growth periods usually happen after a period of difficulties or challenges. If we never have to face challenges, we would most likely not grow in wisdom and understanding. Today I realize that I would not be the person I am, had it not been for the many lessons I learned over the years. Although in the past I reasoned that "God" overdid my schedule for learning as it appeared that before I could take a breath of relief from one challenge I was given another. In time these challenges became larger and more severe. As long as I did not understand how universal laws worked, I received more challenges confirming my belief. The more I became disenchanted about life in general, the harder challenges I was given.

Life seemed an unending task that was full of negative experiences. In desperation I searched for the missing link everywhere but within myself, within my own consciousness that is the part of me, evaluating my world and myself.

When this enormous breakthrough in understanding occurred, my life began to change. This advance is not something that can be taught. It is something that has to awaken within each individual. Today I can only view it as a "previous life span" in which I had much learning to do. Most of my former experiences appear like a "different life" but today I can smile instead of getting angry over that which robbed me of my desired peace and happiness. As long as I believed that the world needed to change, I had struggles to bear.

After realizing that change had to occur within me (meaning my thinking and feeling process), my life became very different. Does it mean that I have no more challenges? No, of course not but the way I handle those challenges has changed drastically. I no longer try to find a source for blame and simply do what it takes to get my affairs in order. If my refrigerator stops working, it won't do me any good to kick it. If my neighbor won't talk to me, I see it as a reflection of his or her state of mind that has nothing to do with me. I no longer entertain guilt feelings wondering what I could have done to make him or her stop talking to me. When we stop reacting to all these believed to be "external" circumstances that are actually "internal" evaluations, we will experience a more harmonious life.

Staying centered on how we interpret circumstances has to do with our own subjective evaluation. It takes practice and a total commitment to change old habits. Why would we change old habits when we are unaware that it is our own habit that is causing the reaction? Old habits keep rearing their heads and we have to make immediate choices either to give them shelf space or replace them with new and more beneficial habits. In time their persistence diminishes and our new habits take hold. Some self-help systems call these old habits "tapes" that keep on playing until we record over them, meaning adopting a new habit.

We are fortunate as human beings and live a more satisfying life when we are able to express greater awareness. Animals also have conscious awareness but theirs is usually called instinct. This instinct seems to be part of a pre-first level of comprehension and is not (has no capability) self-reflective. A cat, for example, will not ponder whether to respond yes or no to a human. His or her life is lived on instinct and not on conscious deliberation. A cat will not make a conscious decision whether s/he should have turned left instead of right. S/he will not worry whether her presence is acceptable to whomever, etc. This level of pre-first-reality understanding was probably prevalent in humans before we had language use. A baby would be considered in that stage before s/he is able to name and choose how to relate to an object because his or her evaluation would not yet be realized as being subjective.

How Do We Change Our Habit Patterns?

Change in understanding occurs from a deep level of universal consciousness where we access our preexisting potential. That is why it is rational to practice feeling attainment before a desired goal happens in actuality. To become empowered means changing the way we think and feel. If we feel lousy, we have to change the focus of feeling lousy into a positive state. Perhaps we have a legitimate cause like the flu, but focusing on the flu is not helpful. We have to focus on total health and also make necessary adjustments to accommodate our body. Resting means restoring the body which can be aided by soft, relaxing music, or positive thoughts (Restoration does not necessarily exclude conventional medicine). Changing feelings is a process that is activated and happens within the person and is not the result of an external procedure. Participating in the process has many benefits as it empowers the individual and eliminates victimhood. Rather than thinking "poor me," we accept that the body's intelligence is trying to tell us to take better care of ourselves.

Where Is the Potential for Change Located?

We have to realize that the pattern of the transcendent is potentially within all creation because there is no individuation from a universal consciousness perspective. This realization is part of third-level understanding and is not comprehended in a first-level materialism. In human consciousness, this unlimited potential is available within a human's conscious awareness that is connected to universal consciousness. Change is not something we can get physically. It has to awaken within us. Yes, we do have options to physical changes such as our wardrobe, house, car, or what to eat, etc., but we are not talking about these changes. We are talking about changes in understanding that happen within us, accepting the potential of the transcendent.

If we use an analogy, we can state that each one of us represents a drop of water that emerged from the ocean but we, as individual drops (human beings), are not considered the sum total of the ocean. Although many drops of water can create a lake or a stream, the birthplace of all drops is still the ocean. No matter how small or how large we become as a body of water, we are still part of the ocean (consciousness). Therefore, the potential for change is located in cosmic or universal consciousness and is encoded in our spiritual DNA, expressed according to our current level of comprehension.

What Happens When Self-conscious Awareness Awakens?

When self-conscious awareness awakens to the realization that evaluation of person, place, or thing is an internal rather than an external process, the birth of a human's conceptual participation (in how s/he relates to his/her reality) happens. Matter is no longer simply an external objective fact, but a subjective process of evaluating its preexisting potential through the vehicle of consciousness. Entering consciously into our "inner" space means participating in a universal consciousness that is never separated from us. We become our own experimenters.

Mindfulness used to take decades to learn, yet today we profit from technology that can assist us in entering into a deeper state of mind in a relatively short period of time. There are hundreds of different methods to help the individual quiet his/her mind by entering into an alpha or theta state. Among the many tools, cassette tapes and CDs are readily available today for enhancing lower cycle brain waves, for relaxation, for clearer thinking, for better health, for reprogramming our habits, for gaining prosperity, etc. Today we recognize how innocent (ignorant) we can be about areas of universal knowledge and the part it plays in realizing our own path to wisdom.

Can Prayer Help Us Change?

Yes, whether we are fully aware of the actual process or not we can use prayer to implement change. Prayers are answered because it is our preexisting potential at work within universal consciousness

(Self) that processes the individual's request regardless of his or her particular religion. Prayers work also regardless of the person's cultural orientation because, at the transcendent level, wholeness exists within every human being. Most humans are not yet aware of this inherent gift because their awareness has not sufficiently developed.

Prayers are not dependent on specific sacred methods, rituals, or ceremonies because if the belief for healing exists it does not matter whether a shaman or a medical doctor performs the healing. The essence of healing comes from the preexisting wholeness believed to be activated through the shaman or the medical doctor. Thus we can state that the successful healer is using preexisting wholeness within the patient to its fullest potential.

If healing depended on a medical doctor only, s/he would have a very difficult task particularly in a first-level understanding since it would depend on his or her own faith and capabilities to do so. What a tremendous responsibility they would have.

With advanced second-level comprehension, we begin to realize that universal laws work whether we are conscious of this interaction or not. When we have gained the understanding of our preexisting potential, meaning that we are never separated from the wholeness of universal consciousness, we will understand the importance of our state of mind.

The reason people often feel better without any medical intervention is that the preexisting wholeness of every person exists whether s/he is aware of it or not. Our belief system determines our self-image and it is our self-image that determines our current level of comprehension. Any support system and love we have in our life will also play a major role in our state of wellness.

This statement does not deny legitimate medical advice. It is simply used to show the spiritual foundation of healing and the difference in level comprehension.

Note: It is our belief that in order to eradicate cancer or other life-threatening illnesses, we have to begin to understand and incorporate the importance "mind" plays in our lives.

Educating people regarding their own psychological dynamics will yield the greatest breakthroughs in medical history.

As we gain greater understanding, we realize that belief is in ourselves and not in authority figures that are external from us. The psychological meaning we ascribe to any situation is symbolizing our current understanding and reflects our behavior. Once we realize where we process our information and our emotions, we can make the necessary changes and we can chose to either react positively or negatively to any situation.

What Is the Difference between Religion and Spirituality?

One interpretation states that religious people are afraid of going to hell and spiritual people have already been in hell and don't ever want to return.

Briefly stated, religion is prescribed dogma. Dogma is frequently created by authority figures, implemented through faith rather than reason. It is generally based on a fundamental set of beliefs and practices that are primarily rooted in an external source, either supporting you or punishing you (God or the devil). It is often believed to be something (or someone) that exists beyond the physical world. Salvation is believed to be fully enjoyed in the afterlife.

Spirituality is uncovering the divine essence that exists in all of us. It is the connection to the beloved, our inner space, the Source of all existence from which we are born. Most of us at first are not aware of this gift. Waking up and making a conscious connection to this Source will entail much personal dedication, significant joy, many surprises, and a different lifestyle. In order to stay centered we have to make time for solitude. Solitude does not mean that we have to live in a cave by ourselves, but what it denotes is that we have to make time to honor the invisible side of creation. It means discovering that God is not a physical form in heaven but is our primary Source of energy or intelligence that is never distant from us. This realization is a most exciting experience as we are connecting with a different God. Not a male or female that is somewhere beyond our view, but an intelligence and energy from which we are never separated.

The realization of this connection is what we could label rebirth. We are actually born anew as an individual with an understanding of the infinite "inner" Source. What a miracle, what a celebration. Nirvana or bliss state will not be something that we chase for fifty years but will be a realization that comes with a paradigm shift in the way we experience and understand the universal aspect of our nature.

Imagine how different relationships between humans will be. Instead of living in anger and frustration, we will rejoice and celebrate each other everyday. Instead of hating, we learn to love. Love is the nectar that heals all wounds. Love is an energy; a vibration that changes the world. You cannot give love when you yourself don't feel loving. We can't give that which we don't have. Learning to love ourselves will no longer be a ridiculous feat or a narcissistic way of living but a means of giving more to the world. When we feel loving, our partners, kids, pets, and even our plants respond accordingly.

Test it yourself. Create a loving feeling and then see if you can include people or things in your world you don't feel loving about. Most likely you will experience a different relationship to the previous (negative) states of thinking and feeling because love is a powerful tool for implementing change. Here is another way for testing this principle. Buy two identical plants and give one special attention by praising it or loving it in some form and ignore the other one. See what happens. You will notice that the plant which received your loving attention will flourish and the one you neglected will either not grow properly or die.

Questioning the purpose of life started thousands of years ago. Each century produced individuals who asked: **Who am I? Where did I come from? Why am I here? What makes me human? Is my death really final?**

By now, you may have realized that the answers to these questions depend on the individual's level of comprehension. Let me provide another overview of how this one question, who am I, would be answered within the three different levels of comprehension.

A first-level interpretation to the answer "Who am I" would most likely be: My name is Paul or Kathy Smith, and I am a white, black, Asian, or Hispanic male or female, twenty-eight years old, and live in Kansas, part of the United States. I am five feet nine inches tall and have black, brown, or blonde hair. I speak two languages, and I am a carpenter by profession.

The conversation might continue with: I have two brothers and three sisters and my parents died when we were young. I am currently married or single and live in a townhouse. I belong to the X church . . . and I am a member of the Y organization.

What this individual shared is information pertaining to his or her level of comprehension. It is composed of facts, places, people, and observations. There is no realization that our physical life contains a spiritual extension. Mind or consciousness plays no part in this first-level comprehension as it is most likely viewed to be synonymous with one's brain. The brain in this first-level understanding acts as a biological part of the individual's body. We could state that there is no capability for the individual to reflect upon the part his/her mental process plays within him or her and there is no realization of the psychological dynamics taking place within this individual. Life is a series of experiences involving different people, various places, and typical or atypical things. This so-called external reality is structured from experiences with people, places, and things and the individual's reality is predominantly based on data that authority figures have established for him or her.

In first-reality understanding, secondhand data from cultural authorities is usually blindly followed and rarely questioned. Traditions and cultural indoctrinations are handed down from generation to generation. Salvation is generally viewed as an aspect experienced in the afterlife, provided the individual lived decently while on this earth plane.

In most cases, God is viewed as a physical or physical-like person residing in heaven. Heaven of course is believed to be a tranquil and loving place beyond the clouds. In this first level of comprehension, there is a perceived separation between God and

God's creations. God is believed to be the supreme ruler, watching every step we make.

Individual boundary lines are predominantly narrow and limit the way in which the individual expresses a realm of possibilities as the importance belief plays in a person's decision-making process has not been realized. Life is based on circumstances that are beyond one's control. Blaming others or blaming circumstances serves as a defense tool that is "external" from the person when justifying his or her life.

In second-reality the answer might be: I am Kathy or Paul Smith, a human being striving to make my life happier and more fulfilling (Most of the above personal information may still be included but this individual will go one step further). I have awakened to the actuality that I have something to do with the way I think and feel and I am no longer a victim of my circumstances. I have learned the importance of self-esteem and my level of self-esteem mirrors my current self-image. The way I think and feel is a subjective process that happens within me and is not, as formerly perceived, a result of someone or something residing outside of me.

I have made a quantum leap in understanding and realize that I function psychologically as well as physiologically and my reality is no longer based on an objective, external world. I have further learned to referee by accepting or rejecting subjectively the interpretation I give to any input from any source and can therefore react or not react to any particular situation. I have realized that all reactions have to do with my internal self-image, and they are not the result of the other person's verbal, visual, or written delivery. For the first time, I understand the importance of how I mentally evaluate all input and realize that I am much more than my physical body.

Knowledge is viewed as a process of learning not only provided by different mentors and schools but by tapping into a preexisting potential which in third-reality has been known as Akashic records, universal consciousness, wholeness, the I am that I am, the Allness, the Kingdom within, Hyperspace, Cyberspace, all-knowing wisdom or God. These are all names for human transcendence, a part of the continuum of an unfolding universal consciousness. Consciousness can be expressed in different levels and the more awareness I have, the faster I can begin to understand the universal laws that are connected with my physical and mental life. I realize that there is a profound difference between religion and spirituality. By nature I already am a spiritual being but may not be aware of this preexisting gift. Religion emerged from dogmas that were canonized by authority figures.

All knowledge already preexists in potential, in universal consciousness, and therefore learning to tap into this potential will provide me with the guidelines and the lessons that were most likely established before my birth by a higher intelligence and/or power. My world is no longer a causal agency which places the responsibility and empowerment within myself, thus creating my own reality. What is real for you may not be real for me, and vice versa. By now I realize that unless a person is aware that s/he is more than his or her physical body, s/he cannot relate to a second level of understanding. In second level, a person's world is realized as a reflection of his or her own level of comprehension. My reality creates my behavior and therefore reflects my level of understanding. The awakening of mind has taken place and the boundaries of my believed world have now expanded. I have gained a better understanding that my beliefs form the evaluations of my world and these given beliefs are predominantly created by being open to preexisting potential within my transcendent Self.

Until I begin to question given beliefs, my reality does not change. As I practice change I am able to help particularly my children understand the important part they play in forming their reality.

Making choices empowers me and although the choices may not always be the best, they can provide further lessons for learning. Life is realized as a school that never ends. My physical existence on this earth lasts only for a short period of time, but my spiritual existence or soul lives on forever.

If we compare universal consciousness or the part that lives on forever with an entire body of water, we can state that I am a drop of this body of water individualized as Margrit, continuing as a drop of water until the time of my physical death. My current level of consciousness (the drop of water) is guided by universal consciousness (the entire body of water) deciding the fate of my future lessons. Life is a series of experiences and circumstances helping me to become a more aware spiritual being. Awakening to greater levels of awareness takes courage and a commitment to experience a world of which we know very little. Change is the only constant in my life and where this change will take me always has a certain amount of mystery. I become a traveler inviting unknown experiences rather than fighting them or being afraid of them.

Fear is not trusting this infinite wisdom called God or a misunderstanding of universal laws. We still need a certain amount of fear in order to respect heights, heat, water, etc., but I am talking about a different fear. It is the fear of finding out who I am, the fear of living a more peaceful life, of living in greater harmony with the universe that escapes first-reality.

In second-reality I am beginning to notice the unwavering accuracy of the existing universal laws. The way I think and feel determines the way my day, week, month, or life is going. I no longer blame "outside" circumstances for what is happening in my life. The more centered I am, the easier my tasks are completed, the fewer people I have in my world that are negative. I have realized that negative people are no longer comfortable in my presence and avoid my company. This means that my circle of friends will change. Negativity attracts more negativity and positive actions attract positive reactions.

As I practice these new principles, my health improves and I feel more empowered and have greater levels of energy.

Blame is realized as a way of hurting myself and is no longer practiced. Shifting out of negative situations (having accepted and internalized negative levels of vibration) becomes a conscious effort, because the ramifications from these negative levels are realized and are now deemed unacceptable. Forgiveness is a path for freeing my own mind from potentially harmful energy. Being continuously angry at someone creates illness. Positive self talk is advantageous as we generally manifest what we think and feel. "That which we fear has come upon us." Changing other people is no longer possible as I realize that, unless the motivation for change is present, they will not change.

Differences in the way first-level individuals work are realized as a reflection of their level of understanding and will no longer be judged. Judgment of others has negative results. A realization that I have something to do with the way I feel has taken place. Life is beginning to be celebrated instead of feared. The realization of human influence is being recognized. The more people we have practicing a peaceful state of being on a regular basis, the more our world will be peaceful.

The more violence we watch in any form or media, the more violent acts we encounter. Second level of comprehension is truly a celebration of the individual's birth as a spiritual human being capable of accessing unlimited potential.

Prayer and healing is realized as tapping into the realm of preexisting wholeness. Although I may still slip into a first-reality habit pattern here and there, I am now conscious of how these habits manifest and affect my life. I can now utilize my newfound wisdom to change these habits. Changing my negative feelings at the onset keeps me from possibly being depressed for weeks or months. This increased level of awareness allows me to referee any situation without judging myself about former habits. I have learned to replace potentially harmful feelings with beneficial feelings. Life has more meaning and is lived more deliberately as I realize that what happened yesterday or years ago cannot be changed but I can change the way I view and react to those situations. There are always exceptions and in some cases I can make amends to situations that pertain to my possible negligence. For situations that were not under my control, I can only view them differently. No matter what happened before, I can utilize the cosmic laws to my benefit and the benefit of others, starting this very moment.

In third-reality, the answer to "Who Am I" would be that I am Kathy or Paul Smith, a spiritual being expressing my beingness in a physical body for a period of years. (Age, height, profession, etc., might still be included but the description of the self is no longer simply an observation of physical facts.) I play an important part in the evolution of all humans and have now realized that the foundation of all existence is universal consciousness from which I am not separated. With God as Source of all creation my conscious awareness is an extension of a unified ground of being from which I will never feel alone again. My life has radically changed because I have now realized that the totality of everything is interconnected. There is no separation between this tree or that dog in consciousness as all are connected to this universal Source expressing their particular level of comprehension (In pre-first-reality the animal is part of consciousness but does not seem to have the capability to be self-conscious or needing to referee.) For the animal, all expressions work from pure intuition, guided by each individual's DNA.

I can understand third-reality principles intellectually long before I can practice them actually. The difference is enormous in the capacity to manifest my dreams. I can read three hundred books about a subject but unless I apply this knowledge it remains simply intellectually stored information. Fully living in third-level harmony is where mystics reign. It is a level that ends all judgment because I realize where judgment takes place (in me) and what it produces. So-called transcendent flow experiences are more numerous where time stands still, where I feel a total connection of all there is, where the individual I is experienced as the universal "I," part of everyone and everything. It is a level where peace and harmony reign, where I am connected with everything and where an "I-thou" perspective is practiced everyday. It is a level in which I consciously practice universal laws and feel them manifest within and without myself. Third-level comprehension has to do with the realization where I understand that universal consciousness is the foundation of our existence that is infinite in expression. The "I" that makes up Margrit is no longer viewed as a separate unit but as an extension of wholeness or universal consciousness including Margrit's world.

My formerly dualistic worldview is now replaced with the monistic worldview in which I am an extension of a universal potential that preexists my conscious actualization. Healing is viewed as connecting with the perfection that already is and prayer is realized as one of the ways of connecting with universal wholeness. In third-reality, I realize that being produces doing. The more I can be in the totality of these universal laws, the more I can manifest its fruits.

Being means being more fully aware of the unfailing principles that govern the universe. Since universal consciousness has multiple levels, it is in first-level ignorance where so-called good and evil is expressed through human language. These dualistic properties are believed to be external from the individual. Evil in second-level comprehension is realized as being ignorant of how universal laws work (Evil has been expressed by Mary Baker Eddy as error some place.) It is difficult to change my beliefs when I am not even aware of the part these beliefs play in determining my life. Limited boundaries or a limited way of understanding living can be explained with the following example:

Imagine a skyscraper with one hundred stories. You proudly state that you are living in the skyscraper on the first floor. You express pleasure for being a part of the one-hundred-story unit, but you do not have the same daily view as the person on the fiftieth floor or the one-hundredth floor. Living contentedly on the first floor does not give you the perspective of living on the one hundredth floor. The view you are enjoying from the first floor is very limited. Although you are a tenant of this large building, the space you occupy on the first floor restricts your capacity to daily view the entire city. Translating this story into levels of comprehension, this would mean that although you may have a satisfactory life in first-level comprehension, you don't know what it would be like to live in second or third-level comprehension. Your scope for realizing different living conditions enabling you to realize an expanded view (level of awareness) does not yet exist. This example serves only as a simplistic metaphor indicating differences in views and reality but does not take into consideration the sheer complexity that is interwoven in consciously living with greater levels of awareness.

How Can You Speed Up the Process of Moving into the Next Level of Awareness?

By becoming more aware of how you think, feel and act, by practicing any form of meditation that evokes at least alpha and/or theta brain waves, and by taking intermittent time for practicing solitude (getting in touch with your inner Self), you can increase your understanding.

The answers are many and it depends again on the level of comprehension that is doing the questioning.

It would not be rational to speed up a process of which I am not aware. A "higher" level of consciousness that many people name "God" has implanted in me the seat for motivation. If there is no motivation or drive for change or exploration, humans remain in the level they are currently expressing. This explains why we can have one hundred students and teach them all the same curriculum, yet the outcome is very different. Some will learn the lessons immediately, and others may never fully comprehend the given material. In order to understand these third-reality principles we have to relearn our ways of being, believing, and understanding. You may wonder why it is so difficult to attain this state of perfection. The answer lies in the capacity to comprehend and being capable of practicing the principles responsible for manifesting desired results.

If we are now capable of producing peace and happiness, this means that we would also be potentially capable of destroying this earth and its inhabitants. As mentioned earlier, universal consciousness contains both spectrums, the beneficial and the detrimental. Universal energy cannot be destroyed; it has to be transformed with "higher" levels of consciousness, fostering peace and love.

Unless we learn the principle laws and apply them accordingly, we could be a potential danger to society. Manifesting either side could be instantaneous and acting without the proper awareness could be fatal. Ask yourself would you like it if your neighbor had the mental capability to eliminate your life, your family, your environment?

As we fully realize these awesome principles, we would no longer implement detrimental applications because we would be aware that the law can only return what we sow. Buying into destruction is very dangerous since it activates that level of consciousness capable of destroying us all. Therefore, simply using the law without truly knowing how it works could be dangerous.

I am living where I am meant to be and as my awareness increases my reality changes. As my level of understanding shifts, I am potentially capable of fully living in harmony with these universal principles.

Why Would I Want to Speed Up the Process of Understanding?

You would only want to speed up the process if you are able to understand the principles intellectually. Otherwise it would not make any sense. Realizing that there is a universal intelligence that is far superior to yours, capable of guiding you beyond your current understanding, is an awesome discovery. The intelligence that questions is the same intelligence that answers and supplies. Finding and living life's purpose brings satisfaction and a greater level of joy and happiness. Our preexisting potential unfolds according to our level of motivation and our current level of understanding.

Why Would I Be Capable of Understanding Third-reality before I Am Ready?

You may be able to understand the principles of third-reality intellectually but knowing this information intellectually does not mean that you can actually practice it.

The fruits of third-level understanding will emerge by practicing the laws governing our entire existence. You would not be able to practice third-reality before you are ready. This readiness unfolds within you and is not something that someone can give you. It is usually a process of much conscious work spanning over time and getting easier as a result of a greater level of awareness.

Questions such as "where did I come from," "why am I here," "what makes me human," "is death final," have been discussed for thousands of years. The answers all vary with the level of understanding that will do the interpreting. If we take the first question, for example," where did I come from," we can state from a first-reality comprehension that I came from the womb of my mother or that God answered my mother's prayers or that the male sperm found the female egg, etc. Although these answers have truth for a person in first-level comprehension, they are missing the transcendent nature that created me in the first place. (I am conscious awareness connected with universal consciousness.) We can get into philosophical discussions that will become enormously complex because, depending from which level of comprehension we view this question, we will have different answers. Without some method for verifying an answer experientially, no answer is more true than the other because it always reflects the individual's level of comprehension. A person conversing with third-level comprehension would have a more inclusive view than one from first-reality understanding because this person is able to test universal laws. The same principles apply for the subsequent questions.

Life is not lived by definition but by experience.

How Do We Attain Enlightenment?

Attaining enlightenment through Eastern teachings means generally practicing meditation. The form this meditation takes can vary from sitting, to chanting, to walking, or breathing in a prescribed way. The individual is asked to participate actively, often with the help of a teacher. Practicing with a teacher can be tricky, particularly when the individual is asked to get rid of his or her ego. Eliminating the belief in separation can be harmful when we believe that we have to destroy our ego in order to gain enlightenment. It takes conscious awareness to follow a master's instructions, and even the Eastern avatar, J. Krishnamurti, rejected this master-follower approach. When the belief is in a Master, the individual is unaware of the part his or her own control plays in the decision-making process. In a first-reality comprehension, we would not be aware of this interaction as it is in second-reality where we discover that our ego is our conscious awareness making our decisions.

Jumping from a mostly first-reality Western understanding to a third-reality Eastern comprehension can bring difficulties as to the importance of the self-image in the individual's decision-making process. In the West, we celebrate high individual self-esteem as this state of being is the function of an individual who is motivated to achieve in his or her world. This sense of achievement, most always, translates into a productive individual who is capable of making a difference in this world. Feeling good about oneself means living healthier and happier. Integrating this spiritual wisdom is best handled with sufficient knowledge about the differences between Eastern and Western approaches. Eastern monistic understanding regarding cosmic truth is not questioned, but the approach for achieving this state of "bliss" needs scrutiny. When we give up personal thinking and acting, we are allowing someone else to direct our life and the end result may not produce the quality of life we had hoped for. This is not to deny helpful people but is simply a form of caution that might eliminate undesirable consequences such as those created by Jim Jones or the leader of Heaven's Gate.

Enlightenment from a Western perspective is realizing the transcendent nature of the human being, including a stage of actualizing personal achievement. Practicing greater levels of awareness can take place anywhere (such as at home, at work, the beach, or the mountains). Tuning in means getting in touch with the quiet space within our transcendent aspect from which we are never separated.

When Did Third-reality Worldview Start?

The awakening of a monistic worldview started in the West in early Greek culture and in small "pockets" has continued to current time. In those early times there was very little challenge to secret societies since 90% of the population did not read or write. The need for secrecy (then and now) was/is to challenge the truth set by authorities. It was dangerous in the past and, in most cases, a sure ticket to execution. Authorities reigned within a dualistic model that worked efficiently because cultures had limited social, intellectual, or financial mobility. This cultural handicap was used by the rulers for thousands of years because they controlled the masses by prescribing what to believe. Instilling fear kept the population more manageable. Within this prescribed form of living, there existed no space or awareness for self-reflection. The motto was most likely survival of the fittest in the way we currently observe survival in our animal kingdom.

When we understand the fundamental basis of monism, we have realized that creation is an expression of the universal source that is also known as infinite wholeness.

The belief is in the believer rather than in the named deity the individual uses to express his or her belief. Instead of thinking that it is God's will or Allah's plan to help or hurt us, we realize that we are extensions of an unlimited potential that works according to our level of understanding. The more we are aware of these existing universal principles, the more we can make use of them. Does this mean that God or Allah could not be helpful? No, not at all, since the potential for the desired help already exists in consciousness, whether we call it God, Allah or universal mind. It is ever present whether we are aware of it or not. This infinite wholeness is the basis of all healing, whether it is physical, mental, or spiritual.

Healing expressed from a third-reality comprehension has to do with the awakening of the individual to this preexisting form of energy and intelligence that is not visible but is capable of being tested. Healing means accepting preexisting wholeness rather than having to learn a solution through some form of doing. With the knowledge that perfection is already contained in universal consciousness (wholeness), we often witness spontaneous healing or what is often referred to as a miracle.

What Is Healing?

A healing is when we relinquish the belief of our own individual limitations and tune into the universal power Source in which everything preexists as wholeness. With this change in focus and understanding, we no longer hold the belief that our Source is individual. With this shift in understanding we are capable of tapping universal wisdom in which healing preexists our acceptance. Healing means replacing our current state of ignorance with the perfection of wholeness. Learning to detach and/or surrender the ignorance of a finite self with an awakened universal Self is the goal of Holographic Psychology.

This interpretation is not yet widely known, but once realized it will change our former belief in limitation forever. Working with nonvisual principles in first-reality is foreign to our way of life, yet these invisible energies can be empirically tested. We soon have proof as our level of awareness, meaning our way of thinking and feeling produces responding results. These results can either be positive or negative as the spectrum of universal forces entails both directions. The end result is based on whether we focus on the preexisting potential or a limiting first-level authority interpretation. Each level will bring justification based on the particular level of thinking and feeling. Remember, our reality is an evaluation process that is based on our beliefs.

Universal consciousness exists in many different levels of expression, and to this day we have no clue how many levels there are. Universal consciousness is governed by laws that express either negative or positive thought, form and feeling. The outcome of situations is based on the individual's level of understanding. When there is no comprehension that we are more than our physical bodies, we are unable to consciously practice a universal principle that entails corresponding laws. It would simply be irrational.

However, the reason rituals and ceremonies work in different cultures is because the healing is not in the method or a particular ritual or ceremony but preexists as unrealized universal wholeness within every individual awaiting actualization.

♥

What Can We Gain from Examining Ancient Sages?

When we examine ancient sages, we can discover proof regarding universal wholeness. The Buddha, for example, is one of these mystics that awakened to the essence of these universal principles.

What Buddha realized was a breakthrough revealing to him the foundation of cosmic consciousness. This breakthrough occurred over twenty-five hundred years ago. Buddha was no ordinary person since he was born as royalty and was therefore taught to be a leader. Having the ability for self-discipline was an enormous benefit and created in him an inner drive to halt human suffering. Caring for the other person was a new experience for Buddha and the art of practicing meditation changed his understanding forever.

Enlightenment was the result of being consciously aware of the existence of cosmic mind as the basis of all creation. This eliminated the belief that humans were created apart from God as separate individuals. The individual is born as a separate and distinct entity but is not separate from cosmic consciousness. In a first-reality orientation, the individual would not be aware of this interrelationship as the needed level of awareness is still asleep. This statement does not make sense until the individual realizes that s/he has a mind (second level of comprehension) that is the same mind as universal mind or third-level comprehension. "Mind" and "consciousness" concepts are used when the individual awakens to his or her transcendent nature.

Perhaps we can state that the Buddha was the first psychologist to realize that wisdom is a function of the individual's mental or "inner" dynamics that is subjective and expresses according to the individual's interpretations. The Buddha earlier and Jesus later all disagreed with the way the authorities handled the culture of the population. For many centuries the ruling authorities were believed to be the sole source of truth.

Many fascinating stories arose from the followers of Buddha. A student pursuing enlightenment asked him, "Are you God?"

His answer was, "No."

"Are you an angel?"

"No."

"Are you a saint?"

"No."

"Then what are you?"

The Buddha answered, "I am awake."

"Buddha" means the "Enlightened One" or the "Awakened One." He taught a religion that was devoid of authority figures or rituals. He argued that "belief in rites and ceremonies" binds the human spirit. It is amazing that it took twenty-five hundred years for humanistic psychology to discover how mental boundaries limit the self-image. Buddha attempted to teach a path that would end human suffering. The end of suffering, however, had to come through individual self-arousal and self-initiative and not through the power of various gods. Salvation had to be gained by personal diligence and not a separate supernatural being. Buddha condemned all forms of divination, soothsaying, and forecasting as he believed that they played no part in attaining enlightenment. His orientation to the world changed drastically after his own enlightenment as he gained knowledge of the universal Self.

For example, pain was subsequently viewed as ignorance of one's cosmic Source. Pain is often the feedback loop of unfamiliarity being practiced. From a first-level comprehension we can find much protest over this statement since the reader can state that if you break your leg there is physical pain. This is absolutely true, but the source of the physical pain originated long before the accident happened. True meaning of this statement comes with advanced second or third-level comprehension.

The Buddha and Jesus were capable of teaching universal principles and were either born enlightened or experienced a transformation within their conscious awareness, altering their understanding after tapping into the wisdom of an all-inclusive Source or universal consciousness.

Although the existence of our physical bodies ends at a particular time on this earthly dimension, our soul connection is infinite and never dies. Imagine how much fear we could eliminate by emphasizing this continuance. Instead of fearing going to hell at the end of our physical life, we would be able to look forward in peace to a different form of existence by practicing a peaceful existence today.

When we retrace history, we become aware that it is the followers of the Buddha who created a religion requiring the worshiping of Buddha rather than practicing enlightenment within themselves. His followers changed his principles into a theistic model and so did the Christians and the Muslims.

It is amazing to realize that Buddha never wrote anything during his lifetime. It took over a century and a half before his spoken words were recorded in writing. Oral memory kept generations informed for centuries. Buddha realized that it was the universal mind that kept everything going and not the believed function of the individual mind. Universal mind operates through the brain of the individual as an extension. Our mind transcends our brain. Our brain is a physical part of our body where mind is an invisible part (transcending brain) of our existence. Recognizing the difference between universal mind and our physical brain is crucial in the evolution of our awareness because our brain will subside when our physical body dies, but our mind or soul will live on forever.

In Buddha's teachings there is never a separate self to be born, to be reincarnated, or to die. There is only conscious awareness that through spiritual awakening of its unlimited potential is continuously manifesting worlds, galaxies, and universes that mystics have called involution or teleology.

With the understanding of this monistic approach, we will no longer feel separated from our universal Source. Feeling lonely will no longer be an issue as the individual will realize that s/he is never separated from preexisting wholeness. This realization will end any feeling of superiority regarding one human "over" the other. All forms of segregation emerge out of the ignorance of one human feeling superior to another.

Why Sacred Texts Have Different Interpretations

People with third-reality comprehension produce literature and teachings (either sacred or secular) that are based on a symbolic meaning, validating the stages of first, second, or third-level functioning. With the awareness of a universal mind or spiritual oneness, divinity of a human nature is realized. This realization is the basis of mysticism that formed a library of knowledge called Gnosis, known in Judaism as the Kabbalah or also spelled Quabalah. These teachings were known as esoteric teachings; however, with a literal interpretation of first-reality, they were considered exoteric.

Initially, the Kabbalah or Jewish mysticism was an esoteric doctrine that was confined to a small group of the elite. After the Jews were expelled from Spain in 1492, it became the authentic voice of a small number of people. In those days, the Kabbalah was considered dangerous for noninitiated people because it would create considerable confusion. This form of secrecy regarding this esoteric knowledge lasted until the eighteenth century. Even today, many Jewish scholars still avoid any theological discussions which might revive mystic thought.

Thus the far-reaching attempts of Jewish mystics to interpret theological meaning of existence in any kind of monism remained unknown, and valuable Kabbalistic manuscripts remain unexplored.

The founders of the Kabbalah purposely kept their knowledge secret. What was made public were the writings of Plotinus (205-270 AD), who believed that all existence emanated from the One. He adhered to the norms of their current authority figures and was, therefore, no threat to their political and theological orientation.

Extraordinary thinkers such as Baruch Spinoza (1632-1677) were excommunicated for their monistic teachings and often had to flee the country because they were labeled troublemakers. Baruch was also called an atheist, which of course he was in the eyes of the Judeo-Christian theistic orientation that applied first-reality belief systems. He was really a mystic from a monistic point of view and was often referred to as "The God-intoxicated man" because he taught that God and nature are one. He had good grounds for being nervous as his predecessor Giordano Bruno (1548-1600) had been executed and labeled a heretic and two more of his friends in Holland were victims of political murder. Many of his works were not published until after his death.

Today we realize that third-reality principles were practiced within many major religions but are still kept secret. For example, the Brahmans of India, the mystery religions of Egypt, and Greece, the Jewish, Christian, and Islam mystics of the West all had access to the Gnosis that enabled them to work within the universal mind principles. However, since their interpretations differed from the orthodox they had to keep it secret because their interpretation had no external God to worship. "Monism" means conscious identification with the unified ground of being; often referred to as the cosmic or universal mind in which separation is an illusion.

How Did We Come to Believe That We Are Separate Human Beings?

There are many theories but perhaps the modern view was established by René Descartes (1596-1650), the French philosopher and mathematician who created a dualistic human view in which mind is believed to be a thinking substance that is separate from matter, which is believed to be a physical substance. Dualism asserts that the universe contains two different kinds of substances: one, mental including subjective thoughts and feelings, and, two, physical substance including the brain and body of humans. These substances exist independently of one another but are joined in the pineal gland in the brain. Science and religion were arbitrarily splitting consciousness, giving science the opportunity to research the world of matter (based on reason), whereas religion was given the world of spirit, mind or soul (based on faith).

Theology, the way it is taught in first-reality comprehension, is based on the belief that the creator and the created are separate beings. Surrendering to an external power is what engenders victimhood, in which the individual vacillated between fear and faith. Both fear and faith were separate powers, were viewed as divine sources that were external from the individual and were either helping or hindering his or her current situation. Many different names were given to these separate powers, such as for example, the god of fertility, of harvest, or rain. In most cultures today these gods are still worshiped wherever dualistic theologies are practiced. God represents good and Satan or the devil represents evil.

What Does It Mean to Experience Nirvana?

There are many interpretations of course and these interpretations are based again on the level of understanding that is interpreting it. We will share our perspective.

Experiencing Nirvana means awakening to the realization that one's Source for anything is universal mind. Every individual and every creation is part of the cosmic Self. Nirvana, like heaven for most Westerners, is a mythic place in which we live happily ever after.

In truth the experience of "heaven" is not a final destination (before or after physical death) but a beginning of a realization of the interwoven connectedness of all existence. Nirvana is generally a state of third-reality awakening in which the individual no longer feels a separation between the individual self and the cosmic Self. Within this cosmic consciousness exist different levels of awareness and whether it is the world of mineral, vegetable, animal, or human, it is all an expression of the same universal mind couched in various stages of perfection. Prior to a level of self-conscious awareness, we label our understanding instinct, intuition, or nature.

How Can We Practice Experiencing the Gifts of Cosmic Consciousness?

First, we have to realize that it is an experience no person can give to us as it has to be activated within the individual self. Today we are aware of numerous ways that help center body/mind for experiencing cosmic or universal mind.

Active meditation has to do with human recognition and capability to consciously participate in his or her transcendent inner space of consciousness. In the West, this capability is the awakening of the individual's "inner" nature that is often called one's self, soul, or mind. This realization leads to the capacity to arbitrate consciously between thoughts and feelings that are beneficial or detrimental. Making conscious choices begins with second-level understanding where the willpower of the individual is activated to consciously change detrimental thinking and feeling to beneficial thinking and feeling. This is what we call actively participating in one's own psychological dynamics.

Instructions to mindful practices, breath control, and gaining a centered peaceful state of mind require a conscious awareness that is mostly connected to Eastern teachings. This information is important to the Westerner as we recognize and work with a personal "I" and a universal "I" meaning universal consciousness. Let us approach it somewhat differently. From a Western perspective, "killing" one's conscious awareness (ego) can bring confusion as it is asking the individual to kill his or her willpower to consciously decide what to practice. Killing the individual self (i.e., getting rid of the ego) can lead to problems, not only in the mental state but also in the physical state. As long as we are not aware of the difference between theism and monism, we can actually, unknowingly, begin to "kill" our physical state of being as a result of misunderstood Eastern teachings. As we realize the essence of monism (third-reality understanding), we no longer have to "kill" our ego since our ego will be viewed as part of the whole playing an important part in our own self-image. When we no longer act as a separate being (i.e., God is separate from me), we realize that there is nothing we need to get rid of other than the belief that we are separate from the universal consciousness and any feelings of unwanted limitation.

On the other hand, when we examine passive meditation in which we let go and let God do the work for us, we often believe that we have no personal responsibility as God is supposed to do "it" without our participation. This approach is another form of theism in which we believe that we are separate from God. It is stated in the Bible that God helps those that help themselves. Letting go and letting God do our work only makes sense when we operate from the theistic understanding in which we are separated from the Source of all creation. In the West, most people function with the theistic understanding in which God is viewed as a separate source. Confusion between the individual self (separate from God) and the universal Self (unified with God) will continue until the individual becomes aware of his or her "inner" dimensions that are not yet located (within the transcendent) while functioning in the theistic understanding.

Altering States of Consciousness Is Not a New Invention

Altered states of consciousness have long been tested and used to attain greater insight into the mysteries of the universal mind. For centuries, natives have ingested certain plants to evoke the gods through them in hopes of obtaining information during rituals for healing or finding particular solutions.

In more recent times Friedrich Anton Mesmer (1733-1815), the Austrian physician, used hypnosis or what he called animal magnetism to change peoples behavior. He became aware that when a person entered into deeper levels of consciousness his or her acceptance level changed. The person actually tapped into preexisting wholeness, and in most cases was not aware of this fact. This deeper level of awareness can be accessed through relaxation and does not require specific drugs.

How Can We Access Altered States Today?

With increased knowledge, we have the benefit of accessing an altered state of consciousness without the use of potentially harmful substances. Advanced knowledge and applications from brain/mind research provide us with tools to enter into different brain frequencies producing altered states of consciousness without drugs or masters. This change can be achieved through meditation, specific music, drumming, and various other methods in a relative short time. With the benefit these different brain states produce, we no longer have to practice sitting quietly for thirty years but can immediately use various tested sounds and frequencies to alter our current state of consciousness. Many people believe that in order to meditate efficiently, they have to be able to completely quiet their chatter or the thinking process that accompanies them when in beta state of conscious awareness. Thoughts exist regardless of our efforts, but when we are capable of going beyond the beta level by entering into alpha, theta, or delta brain waves, we will reap the benefits of this quiet state in our meditation. Changing our faulty beliefs and committing ourselves daily to practicing beneficial feelings will change the quality of our life. Incorporating spiritual practices has benefits we have hardly begun to tabulate.

We have learned today that when we program change on a subconscious level, we get more profound results than by simply verbally stating our desires. It is the acceptance within our subconscious level that forms our habit patterns, defines our boundaries, and determines our current level of self-esteem or self-image.

Wisdom or intelligence is no longer a mere function of testing the individual's IQ but is part of the individual's capacity to test the power of the universal mind from which s/he is not separate. When we realize that everything that has ever been said or thought is in a collective or universal consciousness, we become aware that it is easy to tap into someone else's thoughts or feelings, believing that they are our own.

Global meditation creates beneficial changes because we are all connected to a unified ground of being, also called universal consciousness. Understanding why meditation works differs in second-and third-reality comprehension. In second-level comprehension, the positive effect(s) of a group meditation is believed to be the result of participants focusing on a particular outcome, such as peace or love, where in a third-level understanding the result is realized as acceptance by degree. The motivation to accept within universal consciousness is rendering the desired outcome to the degree the group is able to accept the change they are practicing. The above explanation will not make sense in a first-level comprehension, because the transcendent aspect of a human is not known.

We know today, that a strong person can bring a weaker person up, or a weaker person can bring the stronger (but more vulnerable) person down. We notice this correlation predominantly in sports. When a good player is matched against a poor player, he either improves the poor player or becomes inferior. We can also notice how powerful speakers can influence an audience. The dynamics of a group will change according to the dominate level in control.

How Do We Change an Unacceptable Situation That Is Part of Our Belief System?

Desire for change has to be a priority. Practicing this change takes discipline and an awareness that is capable of differentiating between habitual and newly desired habits. When we have located this realization as part of our subjective functioning, we have gained an enormous leap in understanding. It is the realization that how we interpret anything has to do with our own internal understanding (subjective dynamics), and this understanding is not based on other people, other places, or other circumstances, but rather on our level of comprehension. After second-level awakening, conscious awareness is capable of reflecting upon the desired feelings.

Practicing different options strictly intellectually (in a beta brain state) will most likely not provide lasting change in our behavior since existing habits have to be changed within a universal subconscious level, accessing at least the individual's alpha or theta level. This also means that we have to begin feeling differently about a potentially harmful situation and begin practicing beneficial feelings.

Changing our former habitual reaction takes conscious awareness and a willingness to do what it takes to alter an undesirable habit. Habits do not change easily as most of us can testify. Staying on a weight-loss program has merits in the beginning, but after the novelty has worn off and we have lost some pounds, we often tend to revert to our old habits. We can read many books on how to win at playing golf, but until we practice physically on the golf course, it will only be inexperienced information. Granted it helps to understand the fundamental principles or theories involved, but nothing takes the place of actual practice. Until conscious awareness awakens, it is usually necessary for someone else to direct one's life.

As long as the individual still reacts to his/her circumstances, s/he has not yet awakened to the realization that all experience is expressed subjectively and is based on the level of understanding the individual is currently practicing. As the different level or stages unfold as an awakening universal Self, all forms of expression will be recognized as a consciously unified divine creation.

What Happens When We Discover That the Consciousness within Ourselves Also Exists within Humanity as a Whole?

We will make a quantum shift in understanding. We will realize that each person influences the cosmic matrix and what we do in our home, town, state, or country affects the world. When we are capable of comprehending this interconnection, we will be able to create enormous changes, affecting everyone and everything. We will further become cognizant that our thinking and feeling leaves permanent energy patterns, shifting universal consciousness either in a beneficial or unhealthy direction. It will also become clear why a person in Egypt can come up with the same idea as a person in Canada. Both people tapped into the preexisting universal wisdom bank simultaneously.

We again can give a great deal of credit to:

Carl Gustav Jung (1875-1961), the Swiss psychiatrist and psychologist as he called this universal realization the collective unconscious. His information provided clues to individual personality quirks that exist within the cosmic Self, including all creation and all potential. Jung found that there were patterns in existence worldwide that were being duplicated by people who had no prior knowledge of such existence nor any connection with other people that were expressing the same patterns.

This realization alone could certainly be transforming as we would be able to enter the universal collective mind at will and experience any other person's experience. As with dreams, this would mean that in the universal unconscious realm anyone's experience could be potentially available. Creative people throughout history have tapped this preexisting potential. However, we need to be cautious because we can also tap into negative energy patterns. Have you ever experienced a scary or negative dream in which you were in a fearful situation or with people you had never met before? We believe that not all dreams provide important messages for us.

It is my reasoning that a person with advanced psychic abilities is able to trace or connect with someone else's feelings or deeds.

Psychics (people with advanced mental capabilities) that are able to crack unsolved mysteries would tap into this unconscious realm where every thought, form, and deed(s) is stored. They can deliberately access these universal thought forms, observe them, note the findings and bring them back into their human conscious level.

We know so little about abilities that are potentially available to all of us. We notice that it is of utmost importance that the individual is capable of realizing the different levels of awareness since the outcome can vary between positive and negative experiences. Western cultures have long honored and adhered to empiricism in which the objective experience is believed to be factual. Until quantum physics proved that the experimenter affects the experiment, it was believed that the tester had nothing to do with the test. One of the many research projects involved mice, which were injected with a deadly virus. Half of the mice that were not handled by the caretaker died and those that were stroked and played with lived. Animals will respond to one person but not to another. My white feathered cockatiel used to be an excellent judge of character. He would hiss if the person entering the room was not beneficial to our environment. Cats and dogs have the same capabilities and so do most other animals.

One of my friends would not go out with a particular date unless his dog approved. We have not given the respect to the animal kingdom it deserves. We are intricately linked and the extinction of one animal can mean the extinction of many other animals. The web of life is interdependent and each species plays an important part.

As we become more aware of these intricate links, we will live with a greater respect for all creation. We will also recognize that deductive reasoning prevails even today and is not necessarily wrong, but is very limiting in the realm of what we are capable of knowing. In order to change our situation and belief system, we have to express a motivation for change and learn a different way of perceiving our reality using inductive reasoning.

Consciousness within ourselves exists within all humanity as there is no separation at the universal level, only different levels of comprehension.

Do Humans Have the Power to Choose?

Yes and No

Humans are given choices. They are capable of entertaining options that preexist their actualization. As stated earlier in our research, we believe that levels of comprehension are designated before birth and include the capability for expressing multiple levels of understanding. If the individual's predestined pattern (spiritual DNA) does not contain sufficient motivation to seek and explore, s/he will live within the given predetermined parameters that may or may not resemble those of their mentors. It is possible that an individual with a high level of motivation is given low-motivation mentors. This discrepancy then plays a major part in their spiritual course of learning. For example, an individual with a high motivational level for achieving success would not deliberately stay in poverty after adulthood is reached. Even as a youngster this predestined pattern would surface and s/he would be motivated to find some form of work or pay or have special interest in reading or acquiring knowledge in general. His/her level of motivation would force him/her to look for alternatives and these alternatives would often be very different from those of his or her mentors. If the child were comfortable with his or her mentors, motivation for change would not play an important part in his or her evolution. This is why one family can have numerous children, yet each child has a predetermined destiny to fulfill that includes numerous lessons and challenges. Some of us are challenged to the hilt or so it appears and others simply sail through life without major lessons. We do not yet understand how this destiny is determined but we do know that it is part of both our physical DNA and our spiritual DNA. Despite the presumption that we believe we know and understand much of our existence, we have not even made a dent into the infrastructure that is running our lives. Imagine fourteen billion cells communicating with each other in our brain alone. The complexity with which our systems function to the minutest detail is incomprehensible for our current level of understanding.

I believe that enormous breakthroughs will happen when we are able to communicate from an advanced level of cosmic understanding. Our current theory incorporates three different levels of comprehension such as the behavioral, humanistic, and transpersonal but there may be many more levels.

Waking up to even a second level of comprehension is an enormous breakthrough from the previous first-reality viewpoint in which we blame our environment for our state of being. As we become "mental shape shifters," we will change the understanding of the world as a whole. As consciousness evolves, we will witness new inventions and will come to a level of understanding where we will practice peace on earth and goodwill for all people. My country, my view, my right, my place on earth will be viewed from a different perspective in which we realize that this individuation called "I" is part of a greater Source from which we are never separated. Caring for ourselves will include caring for others. With this win-win plan we can wipe out wars, hunger, racial, cultural and gender discrimination, disease and negative states of being.

In level two we discover the mental realm or consciousness existing within ourselves. A realization dawns that the world is a feedback loop based on how we evaluate our own thoughts and feelings which express according to our current self-image. It is the discovery that our own psychological dynamics were hidden in first-level comprehension.

In third-level comprehension, we no longer dwell in problems because the connection of all forms of life is comprehended as an extension of a universal level of understanding. We (as conscious awareness) can still vacillate between levels, despite intellectually understanding the principles involved. Living fully in a third-level comprehension will eliminate misunderstandings and life will be realized as heaven on earth. When we no longer exhibit negative reaction to the "outside" world (awakened second-reality), we will live within the understanding of our "inner" world mirroring the "outside" world. This does not mean that we have to sit quietly all day and meditate, but what it means is that we focus our attention on a Source existing within us that is unlimited in its potential, producing both the desire and the method for change or actualization.

Early levels of comprehension will no longer be realized as right or wrong but merely as limited levels of understanding. The more awareness we gain, the more we realize how important it is to stay open to the unknown. As we operate from a greater balanced state of being, our peaceful "inner" state produces a peaceful "outside" environment. The same principle is true for negative thoughts or feelings. In my experience, it appears that if we are not continuously/consciously aware, a slip into negativity can rapidly develop in a hole from which it takes much focus and willpower to climb out again. Negativity attracts more negativity, and a vicious cycle is easily activated. We can forget that feeling and meaning can only be experienced subjectively.

Our life will never be the same when we realize that all things emanate from the one or the world soul. This happens through the intellect where the human imagination can consciously participate in awakening to its divinity. A human's soul can imaginatively reflect the cosmic mind and with this insight actualize spiritual emancipation. Working from a physical-only realm keeps the door to the cosmic realm closed.

Turning inward means practicing some form of solitude. Getting in touch with our "inner" wisdom means focusing away from noise and distractions. This "inner" knowledge of the absolute (also known as Gnosis) is capable of being discovered within each individual as it demonstrates the individual's level of comprehension.

Conscious identification with the unified ground of being is often referred to as cosmic or universal mind, in which separation is an illusion that was created through the use of language while understanding expressed early levels of comprehension.

Do we have choices? The answer is yes, after awakening to a reflective second-reality. We can choose whether to react or not to a person, place, or thing.

The answer is no in first-reality because we react to a conditioned brain that automatically responds to input.

What Changes When Our Awareness Increases?

As paradigm shifts occur, meaning, words, and concepts used to describe reality are no longer fixed in our orientation because the representation will be realized as a function of the individual's conscious awareness. This awareness is based on the evaluation process the individual is using and is expressed according to his or her current level of use (his/her conceptual meaning) which is psychological. With this added realization, it is only natural that when comprehension changes, meaning changes.

Dictionaries convey a word meaning that establishes a system of belief for first-reality understanding. It is clear that in order for a culture to function, we have to have a common language to establish certain rules. For example, for heavy traffic to flow smoothly, we have to obey the traffic lights designating the right of way. We have to be able to identify potential danger and perform certain duties. Clearly, all these measures perform necessary functions on this earth plane, but as an individual awakens to his or her own psychological dynamics, a new set of meanings is established.

As our awareness increases, the fundamental meaning regarding the purpose of traffic lights does not change, but our reaction to red lights changes. We will no longer be impatiently cursing a red light as we realize the part they play in traffic control for everyone.

In the past, for the majority of people, the true meaning of life was not a subject of discussion at the dinner table, as physical survival took precedence. Having a warm place to stay and food on the table was of primary importance.

Again, when awareness increases, we will no longer be victims of external circumstances, other people, places, or things. We will have realized that any evaluation has to do with our own internal thoughts and feelings and that we determine whether to react or not react to any situation (The boss can no longer make me angry as I realize where the anger is located, namely, in me.) Increasing our awareness means shifting our level of comprehension and realizing the inclusion of everything. It means expressing a healthier, happier state of mind, which will produce a healthier lifestyle benefiting the whole world.

With this brief overview, we can notice that the search for a meaningful spiritual life (God) is not as simple as we believed. If I ask you, Do you believe in God? The answer can be, Which God? If I ask you, Do you believe in the Holy Scripture? The answer can be, Which Holy Scripture? If I ask you, Do you believe in truth? The answer can be, Which truth?

As we enter the next century, these different approaches to God realization will become clearer. As stated, the meaning of any understanding is based on the level that is doing the evaluation which, in turn, fits the particular level that is doing the interpreting. If we work from an orthodox view, we have the "right" answer, and if we work from any other view, we also have the "right" answer. You may wonder how everyone can be right. Simple. They are right within their particular level of understanding. For example, you would never tell a Mormon or a Baptist that they are wrong about their particular belief. Within their level of understanding, their truth is right for them.

With advanced levels of understanding comes the realization of freedom to express options and the elimination of negative reactions. Differences are no longer right or wrong. They simply expose the particular level of understanding. From a second-reality understanding, judgment is a feedback loop of the individual's current level. World religions are only reducible to specific dogma when we have no understanding that how we interpret any religion is based on our current level of comprehension. Commenting about God in first-reality would elicit a different response from a second- or third-reality understanding.

How Was Our Belief System Created?

For the West, both Jewish and Christian belief systems became the vehicle for validating all three realities. Further studies will prove that what Jesus reported and what so-called Christianity did with his teachings differs greatly. Early Christianity was primarily used as a political power and secondly as a theology. Fear of going to hell had enormous power over the general population (and still does in many first-level cultures). People in general were told by the clergy how to act and misbehavior entailed stiff punishment. We know today that multiple interpretations existed before and after the death of Jesus. What humans did with his so-called reported teaching has to do with whether the interpretation is based on his nature as being human, as being divine, neither, or both. Humans have always disputed differences regarding the founder of a religion, and unless humans comprehend levels of awareness, they cannot understand these differences.

Realization of these multiple levels of understanding and their interpretation has taken countless centuries to come to fruition. Science suggests that the planet earth is about five billion years old. People recognize physical evolution and the awesome changes that formed geological history. However, few people are aware of human evolution. By that we mean the evolution within human beings including their mental and spiritual realms. The evolution of consciousness is a major part of Eastern theologies but not a part of Western theologies. Only after an individual becomes consciously aware that s/he is basing his or her life on what s/he believes s/he knows about her/himself and others can s/he be psychologically aware that s/he is practicing a worldview of beliefs rather than physical facts.

Life will validate what we believe and will expose our level of comprehension by the way we behave. Our psychological dynamics reflect how we acquire meaning and how individuals respond to world affairs as a reflection of their own evaluation. This is the thinking process with which we encode words and decode them into behavior. Awakening to the realization of a self-conscious human nature is fairly recent and is often confusing because the question of whether a human is finite or infinite may not be fully grasped. In a first-reality understanding, we have the belief of a finite nature as there is no awareness of a consciousness existing within us. After we awaken to the multiplicity of realities, we can entertain differing reports. Until a human understands how s/he acquires knowledge, there would be no way to entertain a comparison in interpretations.

After this acquisition (a shift in consciousness occurs), the individual realizes that his or her data is formulated and interpreted psychologically rather than based on external circumstances. With an "outer" orientation the individual has to believe that all reaction is based on a world that is external from them. This individual is unaware that the truth they "see" (first-reality) is based on data that authority figures have taught them regarding what is right and what is wrong.

Awakening to our mental capacities brings with it a transformation that will change our understanding forever. We believe that there is no ceiling to how far we can go after shifting our understanding. Life is a school and the lessons are never ending.

With a second-reality-understanding, we realize that we are capable of making choices (refereeing) and that we can either practice unwanted feelings or replace them with positive feelings. As we begin to live completely in a state of harmonious flow, we will no longer react to unacceptable experiences nor be attracted to them.

What Does It Mean to Live a More Fulfilling Life?

First and foremost, we must have gained a greater level of awareness in which we realize that our existence on this earth plane extends beyond our physical or material world. Living in peace and harmony takes a reflection that reaches beyond the personal "I." The personal "I" is that which makes diversity within unity, and this unity is contained within universal consciousness. Feeling happy is an inner state that, when animated, will shine like a beacon. The happier we are, the brighter the light will shine. Feeling joy will be a conscious practice that keeps returning to us in ways we may have never dreamed possible. Time is a reflection of the present moment we can make meaningful. Walking our talk or speaking our truth has become second nature, and we are no longer intimidated by others. The more we can be who we are at the core of our being, the happier our life will be. When we understand the location of our comprehension, negative comments are viewed as the reflection of the person stating them. Living a more fulfilled life comes with greater wisdom. Greater wisdom emerges generally with more years of life experiences, and these life experiences are part of the lessons we have come to learn. I do not believe that there is a final stage in learning as there is so much universal wisdom we have not begun to tap.

Taking care of the self does not mean excluding others, but we can't give or share what we don't have. We have to nurture the essence of our being. When we feel happy, we share our happiness with others. Living a more meaningful life has many variations, and it is these variations that are embedded and expressed according to our physical and spiritual DNA.

Living a more meaningful life means no longer getting upset over circumstances or verbal abuse because a reflection has awakened in which we realize where our thinking and feeling originates.

Living a more peaceful life means restoring and maintaining an inner sense of worth that reflects our outside world. When we feel peaceful and happy, our world will reflect that state of being. People we meet and interact with will mirror our sense of being (our state of inner reflection).

Living in darkness or living in a depressed state of being happens when we do not allow divine light to shine through our body. As we gain greater awareness, the "inner" door opens and the beacon of universal love can shine through us. The more we are in tune with universal principles; the more will be revealed to us. Magic as well as uncertainty will accompany our lives, and instead of fearing this uncertainty, we are able to welcome it. Feeling guided means feeling secure, living with more conviction and a trust (in God) that is unfaltering.

We do not have to give up our comforts, only our mistaken beliefs that our lives are based on external circumstances. Living more meaningful lives means adding greater meaning to our understanding and accepting people as they are. The extent of the fullness of life can be a great adventure.

Life is lived with more gratitude and an increased sense of awe for nature and its tiniest creatures as they all play an intricate part in our lives. Living in harmony with nature becomes an automatic response.

Living with more awareness means loving and respecting our body. Life reflects our level of understanding. Fulfillment is no longer based on a material world but on a realization that our innate potential is practicing actualization.

When we live with a greater sense of purpose, we become more creative, and this creativity brings more excitement into our lives.

We can even have fun with a visual element in the sky. Have you ever attempted to make a cloud disappear? It works. Next time pick a small cloud and focus your total attention on that cloud. Silently (or out loud) ask it to disappear. It will. Remember, we are all connected. Living with more awareness changes the reality of the individual and brings with it a clarity that was not previously available.

"Meaningful" is still a subjective term, and what might be meaningful to you, may not be as meaningful to me. As we celebrate the diversity, we can also begin to count the many blessings life has to offer. We partake in life to the degree we are aware. Claim the potential that is waiting to express within you.

Let me share a poem that just came to me:

Don't assume,
Begin to bloom.
All seeds are hidden within you.
Partake in the nectar of eternal youth
By learning about the cosmic truth.

What Is the Most Important Aspect of Holographic Psychology?

We do not live a life based on physical principles governing an objective world. Our lives are guided by a spiritual DNA that unfolds according to its plan. There is a preexisting potential awaiting actualization.

We are the creators of our own myths because all interpretation is psychological and has to do with the level of understanding the individual is currently expressing. This means waking up to our inner potential within universal consciousness from which we are never separate. Location of Comprehension or Feststellung is one of the most significant aspects in this teaching.

Another exciting factor is the realization that we have a preexisting potential awaiting actualization already within us. How this potential will unfold is not known, that it will unfold is certain. Most of us would like to have this assurance. But this will not unfold until we start to live every moment more consciously, practicing peace and happiness. Then we will discover a life of peace and happiness. Creating goals allows us to focus with a greater sense of self-esteem and conviction that is activated more frequently after a second-level comprehension. It is the basis of numerous self-help systems teaching individual responsibility and empowerment.

Organizing specific goals in third-reality comprehension means practicing the gifts of already-existing wholeness. Life unfolds via our biological and spiritual DNA, and our desired or undesired manifestations are demonstrated by our level of comprehension. The individual "I" is realized as an extension of the cosmic "I" where all creation is contained as a preexisting potential. This concept is difficult to grasp and may not make any sense to a reader in first or early second level of comprehension.

Learning and applying the principles of third-reality will be the greatest discovery regarding humans in the twenty-first century. It will change this planet forever.

How Will the Knowledge of Holographic Psychology Change the World?

The information regarding Holographic Psychology does not change the world until the principles contained within it are practiced and integrated into daily living.

When awareness awakens to unrealized potential within one's own consciousness, the importance of conscious refereeing will be practiced. A decision will be made about habits that are either acceptable or need to be replaced. Change is a form of practicing that which the individual desires, and when the belief is activated, s/he will be able to demonstrate his or her fantasized dreams. Awakening to universal mind ranges from actualizing unrealized potential to practicing limitation. The spectrum of consciousness contains both. Our demonstration for either potential or limitation is generally based on the level of comprehension and individual acceptance; either we practice limitation or we practice abundance. We may be practicing either side without being consciously aware of it. In that case, our reality always reflects our belief.

If parents, for example, keep encouraging their children and tell them how special and talented they are, they will perform differently from parents who tell their children that they won't amount to anything. This constant verbal repetition creates a form of subtle programming and becomes a belief, e.g., "I am not smart anyway, I can't do this," or on the other hand, "I can do it if I keep on trying." Changing beliefs takes awareness and the motivation to practice different thoughts and feelings. It is difficult if not impossible to practice abundance when we have no concept of how these laws work. Wishing that you were rich is not practicing feeling rich. It is possible, however, to practice a belief without ever knowing the dynamics behind it. In order to win, we have to practice a winning attitude. The motivation for change has to be present in the individual in order to manifest desired changes.

Unless habits are changed, the individual will operate with the same belief that was instilled in him or her by parents or mentors bringing the same results. Therefore, practicing change consciously will alter the existing pattern of beliefs and in time will replace the old, perhaps faulty way of thinking, feeling and acting. The results of this principle are witnessed best among the competition of sports. Creating high levels of self-esteem and self-confidence has made enormous differences in the overall performance of a team. In order to win, one has to have a winning attitude. Reading about this information will not change the world, but living with greater levels of awareness will, because when we realize that our thinking and feeling determines our quality of life, we will be much more careful in our choices. When we enhance the positive, everyone wins.

How Can This Holographic System Gain a Greater Acceptance?

In order to gain a clearer understanding, we have to think and act in global terms. Knowledge has to be made available to everyone seeking a better understanding. Global education means having a better understanding or functioning on a "higher" level of vibration that is contained within consciousness. The effort to educate the masses will change the generations building our future. With more awareness, we will have more cooperation and more respect for our planet, which also plays an intricate part in our survival. What we label "future" is of course the sum total of our current thinking and actions.

In universal consciousness there is no past and no future as everything exists simultaneously, meaning now. Everything that has ever happened is recorded and exists somewhere in consciousness, and everything that is going to happen exists already in potential. This might be difficult to grasp particularly when we are only oriented to a material world that has a beginning and an ending. This dualistic concept was most likely formulated so that the masses would be able to work within a system that was comprehensible. This linear dualistic construct is not wrong but is limiting in the realm of all possibilities, including the invisible intelligence called consciousness. The importance of consciousness is not yet known to the largest segment of our population as their belief still rests in an objective or materialistic world. This materialistic world was fabricated with the help of science, which separated mind from body in order to work freely without restrictions or interference from the religious authorities. Working in a controlled environment with rats and pigeons is, of course, much easier than working with humans since humans have a capability animals don't have (or to our knowledge don't have), and that is to be able to reflect upon their own actions. Animals work mostly from their instinct, which is innate and demonstrates according to their DNA.

How Do We Gain True Knowledge?

True knowledge has to unfold within the person and is not something that someone can purchase. Granted we can become more knowledgeable with the help of mentors, books, CDs, audio, and video tapes, but knowledge has more to do with an exposure of consciousness of the perceiver, relating to wisdom. We can't buy enlightenment. It is a process that happens within us and has to do with the realization that we are more than our physical bodies. It is recognizing the awesomeness of universal mind expressed as preexisting potential. All knowledge already preexists in potential, and accessing this knowledge has to do with increasing our own level of awareness. As this universal consciousness evolves, so do the people. If universal consciousness were not evolving, we would all still live in caves. What an incredible journey to unlimited discoveries! We can speed up the process of enlightenment by gaining a greater level of awareness, but without this advanced level of understanding (paradigm shift), we would not be able to grasp the dynamics involved.

Functioning in a third-level reality is being in touch with all existence simultaneously. We are never separated from the laws; we may just be ignorant of how these invisible laws govern our existence. As we enter this next century, many of these laws will be better understood.

Third-reality is not a final destination but an exciting and beneficial beginning of a more intelligent existence. How far we can go is anyone's guess. We know so little and pretend to know so much. Third-reality is where I witness the inclusion of everything and everyone.

When we tap into third-reality principles, we notice that our life appears to have more "miracles".

Synchronicity (coincidence) has become a buzzword in metaphysical teachings. Synchronicity happens when we work consciously within the spiritual laws. There are no accidents and when we surrender to this awesome intelligence, we will be guided and will witness multiple forms of so-called synchronicity. We may be looking for a person with a particular talent and meet that person during a special occasion or an ordinary meeting. We may have a need for a particular thing and our neighbor might knock on our door asking if we could use this particular thing. There are many more examples of synchronicity but for now these two examples will suffice.

Advancing human understanding is not something that will take place in the laboratory by pretesting mice or rats. Instead, it will be fostered by researching human potential. In Western civilization, it is difficult to ask someone to experiment with an aspect that is invisible yet it is the foundation of everything. This invisible aspect is what we call consciousness. Learning to unleash this preexisting potential will create the Utopia humanity has dreamed about for centuries. It will also change the way we live as we will understand the foundation of our own existence. We will no longer see ourselves as limited separate beings but as extensions of a cosmic universe. We can continue to name the Source God in sacred terms or call it collective consciousness in secular terms. When we speak of the Self, we mean the unlimited potential or Source of all creation. Consciousness has many names, and these names correspond to either Eastern perspectives (like Buddha and the atman of the Brahmans), or Western perspective where we label it God, Source, the unlimited potential, universal consciousness, collective unconscious, the One, I Am that I AM, Divinity, Wholeness, the Source of creativity, the almighty force, just to name a few.

As we enter the twenty-first century, the wisdom of sages from earlier centuries can be utilized because we are now capable of synthesizing the legacies they left us. This capability will create teamwork and cooperation of unknown proportions. Hate and war will be replaced with love, happiness and cooperation. Accessing creative states of consciousness will be taught before kindergarten and will benefit everyone.

It is my hope that much of today's speculation will become a realization of the awesome potential that is part of our divine nature. Finding ourselves is learning to cultivate the invisible forces that exist within all of us. For best results, this education has to start when a child is young and pliable, and must continue throughout life.

Realizing a potential that is unlimited in scope is available to everyone. Again, the degree to which this potential unfolds is based on the motivational patterns we have been given through our spiritual DNA. We still need diversity, and this diversity allows us to enjoy different lifestyles and professions. Imagine what the world would be like if everybody were an engineer. We would have the most precise lines, directions, compilations, and perhaps mathematical equations, but we would not have anybody to raise and process our food, etc. Accepting greater diversity (such as different customs, different races, or religions) comes with increasing our level of awareness. When we stop condemning that which we are not familiar with or that which does not fit our particular bias, we will experience a freedom that will liberate the world. Orthodoxy as we know it today will only be practiced in the future by a very small minority. We are already noticing a diminishing church population where clergy adheres to a dogma that no longer serves the changing world. This includes misinterpretations of scriptures that Jesus and other avatars taught.

It is our hope that the reader will have gained a greater perspective of so-called "future" possibilities. When we realize that we create the "future" right now, we will be more careful of what we think and feel.

Be careful of your thoughts

Your thoughts become your words.

Be careful of your words

Your words become your actions.

Be careful of your actions

Your actions become your habits.

Be careful of your habits

Your habits become your character.

Be careful of your character

Your character becomes your destiny.

—Anonymous Author

When change or actualization is oriented to preexisting potential, it awakens a process within the human that is empowering and changes the world.

Author

Margrit Spear, PhD/MFT

Margrit Spear holds a PhD in Counseling Psychology from the University of Humanistic Studies in San Diego, California. She is a psychotherapist, a California-licensed marriage, family and child counselor, researcher, and life-coach.

She is currently vice president of LA CCRS, an independent research group that for almost fifty years has been examining the interrelationship between body, mind, and spirit. Her association with the president of LA CCRS, Dr. James Pottenger, began twelve years ago.

Born in Switzerland, she has a multicultural background and enjoys diverse approaches in the field of psychology, philosophy, and religion.

Her professional experiences include research and development for the National Institute for Mental Health for the homeless population, schizophrenics, drug addicts, and alcoholics; working as crisis counselor, academic and psychological counselor for a local college, and lecturer for multiple school projects; developing self-esteem programs for students and administrators; private practice; and owning and operating a retail business. She is also a staff trainer, artist, poet, and ordained minister.

She is the creator of two CDs:

1. *Virtual Healing*, which provides the listener with a new experience combining virtual audio sound and healing potentials that already preexist in universal consciousness.
2. *Positive Patterning While You Sleep*, an all-night CD that has sixty-four statements for positive health, happiness, good relationships, increased self-esteem, and financial success while you sleep.

For more information check out the website at: *www.simplyjoy.com*